The Double Cross

PAUL OESTREICHER

Darton, Longman and Todd
London

First published in 1986 by
Darton, Longman and Todd Ltd
89 Lillie Road, London SW6 1UD

© 1986 Paul Oestreicher

ISBN 0 232 51705 3

British Library Cataloguing in Publication Data

Oestreicher, Paul
  The double cross.
  1. Christianity
  I. Title
  200   BR121.2

  ISBN 0–232–51705–3

Phototypeset by Input Typesetting Ltd, London SW19 8DR
Printed and bound in Great Britain by
Anchor Brendon Ltd, Tiptree, Essex

In memory of Else,
a grandmother whose love
no holocaust could consume

and for Lore, without whom . . .
and her children, and mine

Contents

Acknowledgement

The lyrics of 'Bird of Heaven' and 'Lord of the Dance' by Sydney Carter are quoted by permission of Stainer & Bell Ltd.

1

Sales or Management

Despite the near impossibility of being a Christian, these reflections, these fragments from the life of a reluctant priest and an uneasy Quaker, focus on 'the love that will not let me go'.

Every day Calvary, reflected on every television screen around the world, casts its shadow, one cross and many crosses, over our threatened planet. And who's to blame? Poet, prophet, song-writer Sydney Carter says what many people feel: 'It's God they ought to crucify, instead of you and me, I said to the carpenter, a-hanging on the tree . . .' When, as a young BBC producer in the early sixties, I wanted to get that song on the air, I had a fight on my hands. It would offend too many good Christian listeners. 'So the scandal of the cross is not fit for broadcasting!' I argued. I needn't have been so belligerent, with so gentle a radical as Roy McKay in charge of religious programmes. He knew about the offence of the gospel. His pacifism had cost him his public school chaplaincy during the war.

So, *Friday Morning* was broadcast, with the predictable complaints about blasphemy from some of the 'pillars of the Church'. Familiar enough to Jesus, only in his case they didn't stop at letter-writing. It got very bloody, stirred up by the religious leaders.

The thief, hanging on a cross next to that of Jesus, is no fool to accuse God, but little does he know who it is that's being killed beside him. God himself? Now that this 'man for others' had obviously been defeated, his friends were no longer quite so sure. Anyway, most of them had fled. Peter, their leader, was by now paralysed with fear and guilt. Only one of the inner circle of twelve was there. The one closest to the heart of Jesus. Effeminate, is how many men might well describe John, as though femininity was some kind of disease. Significantly, the women around Jesus had not fled. If there is a weaker sex, it is certainly not theirs.

If there is a God who is reflected in his creation and, mysteriously, in each of us, then anyone with compassion and a sense of justice must feel with the condemned robber who puts all the blame where it seems to belong: on God. Like a lamb, Jesus – in whom his friends recognise God – accepts the world's verdict:

> God is led to the slaughter
> The just redeems my loss
> He shall drink of the torrent's water
> And he shall be nailed to a cross
> (Henri Ghéon)

What better symbol than that for a world struggling for some kind of peace, some kind of justice, a world that's dying to live. At Coventry Cathedral, where I work, it's said with a cross of nails, made from the ruins of war but standing for much more, for a world of torture and hunger, a world where children are shot and villages bombed by men who fear to lose the trappings of power. Yet, quite unnoticed, flowers bloom in arid deserts and love survives in cold climates.

Have the churches, using the powerful slogans of Christmas, Easter and Pentecost which put the cross into context, been playing a sustained confidence trick on the human race? Have we been double-crossed for close on two thousand years by the spokesmen of religious institutions that have almost eclipsed the rebellious young healer and preacher from Nazareth? Jesus was executed for threatening to bring down the religious leaders from their thrones. And perhaps the secular ones too. If he was a threat to the power and credibility of religion then, why not now?

As the Madonna of the Flames runs from the ruins, holding aloft her dying child in silent protest at the holocausts of our world, these and even harder questions remain unanswered. If, in these fragments of recalled and recounted life, there are intimations of an answer, it is not by my design. It is a reflection of the love that endures all things, that will not let me go, be it in the face of terrorists or their accusers, torturers or their victims, rulers or 'their people', servants or their masters; be it in Manhattan or Blackheath, Nazareth or Kalinin, Prague or Windhoek.

My canvas may be large and my journeyings far-flung. But the people – and only they matter – are never larger than life. They can only pretend to be. They all matter equally, hard as it is for any of us to act as though that were true. As Yip Harburg wisely wrote in another context: 'No matter how high or great the throne, what sits on it is the same as your own.' There is nothing in the experiences that I try to share that does not belong in every street, every house, every heart.

What does the cross mean to the man and the woman in the streets of our world? To a few, the sign of contradiction that it is. To some, not a few, a symbol of oppression or even a weapon of war, in the teeth of its claim to liberate and reconcile. To many others a mere ornament, stripped of its horror, turned into a piece of pretty jewellery. Even that trivialisation of the death of God is as nothing compared with its rococo glorification by the Church.

Is there still some way of rescuing the true from the false crosses that have, for so long, contributed to the distortion of our society. Can the cross be rescued from centuries of misuse? Perhaps it can, in molten stone, after the nuclear blast, in a ruined Nagasaki church.

If there can be forgiveness for Pilate and the soldiers who crucified Jesus, is there also hope for the religious leaders who delivered him into Pilate's hands? If there is forgiveness for the persecutors of the Church, the killers of Stephen and of Martin Luther King, if Hitler and Pol Pot and Stalin and Botha – in their invincible ignorance – are not beyond the reach of divine compassion (and heaven help us if they are not, for we are all of the same flesh and blood), then what of a Church that claims to be Christ's Body and in its long bloody history has crucified others rather more often than it has itself been crucified?

The processional crosses that precede princely prelates in high hats and solemn costumes may be as harmless as the Beefeaters in the Tower of London, but in the Crusades crosses broke infidels' skulls and in the pogroms of Good Friday the sign of the cross was a sentence of death to any Jew who was caught by marauding Christians. It is not for nothing that world Jewry is outraged at the idea of a Catholic Order opening a house of prayer on the site of Auschwitz.

Yet to this day the greater part of the Christian Church parades itself as the ark of the truth, the bearer of God's Word. Even after Auschwitz. And in most of its mutually exclusive branches. The Church washes its hands of its guilt and projects it on to its members. And then there is always some excuse, some theological apologia for its betrayals. Sadly, Communists in power have been good imitators of this form of corruption.

Would that this were simply an intemperate outburst of spiritual exasperation, an obsession with guilt. It is not. We are bound to ask whether the cross and what it signifies to a largely unbelieving world is still capable of rehabilitation. All that follows in this little book is an attempt to hear that question without giving way to despair. As, year after year, the victims of Hiroshima and Nagasaki continue to suffer and to die, could we do any less, knowing that the bombers delivering their deadly load were sent on their way with Christian prayer, but not for forgiveness?

It is a little too easy to seek refuge in the knowledge that none of this is true of the saints and martyrs of Christian history who have lived and died with Jesus, the Man of Sorrows, poor, spat upon, tortured and rejected, more often than not by most of the Church. Without their stories we would be very poor. Their spiritual significance cannot be exaggerated. It is entirely relevant to the rehabilitation of the Church, but to argue from the exceptional as though it were the norm is fraudulent. The Church of England, for example, did not really contribute to the liberation of the slaves in the nineteenth century. Wilberforce and his prophetic friends won that battle despite the bishops and their established friends.

At least since the Enlightenment the idea has been abroad in European culture, sometimes implicitly, sometimes explicitly, that the Churches have all along been taking us for a ride. The moral and philosophical case against religion in general and the Judaeo-Christian tradition in particular is strong and has not really been demolished. But people are bored with that kind of debate. Organised religion remains freely on offer. Most people simply choose not to take the offer up. That does not make them knaves or fools. Are they offered the bread of life – or a stone?

Neither goodness nor perversity are the monopoly of any one group of people. Most have certainly stopped looking in any one direction for a solution to the world's problems. All ideologies are suspect. But if justice and peace and harmony with the environment are the needs of the future, anyone with a knowledge of the past is hardly likely to expect religion to come to the rescue. It is not by chance that Northern Ireland is both the most religious part of Britain – by far – and the most violently divided.

There is a branch of Christian learning called apologetics. It is just what that word suggests: presenting the gospel in the most favourable possible light. It is, with the best of motives, the craft of Christian salesmanship. At least until recently the man in the clerical collar has been thought of by most people as a commercial traveller for one of the many varieties of the Christian God. Now that even many of the Pope's frontline troops have, to his regret, gone into mufti, spotting God's emissaries has become more of a challenge.

An Anglican bishop, now dead, told the story of a dramatic flight from New York to London. Air pockets began to shake the plane violently. A woman, believing that disaster was at hand, shouted to a nearby priest, quietly reading his breviary: 'Father, is there nothing you can do about this?' 'I'm sorry, madam,' came the reply, 'I'm in sales, not management.' Such a refusal to panic might have been just what was needed at that moment. But, sadly, the answer was characteristic of the Churches in general. Their paid-up full-time agents, the clergy, tend to play the role of the amateur salesman. The slogans commending God on church notice-boards would be enough to make an advertising executive cringe. In Britain at least, despising professionalism, the Churches make a virtue of not being able to afford Saatchi & Saatchi. Not so on the other side of the Atlantic where financial success is held to be a proof of God's approval. There, God is in direct competition with Disneyland – and doing well. The electronic Church is thriving and may, like Hollywood, blaze a path to the White House. The main-line Churches, Rome to the fore, do not much like the razzmatazz, but seldom is the jet-setting priest's contention seriously challenged, that the Church *is* in sales, not management. God himself, it is assumed, is the Director General and has everything under control. All human effort is, at most, middle management. The Church's essential task is to make sure that the boss is treated with due deference: 'worshipped and adored' is the proper terminology. There are priceless rewards.

I am not into the business of apologetics. The successful salesmen are not my models. In fact – and that may make me a poor parson – I am most decidedly not into sales at all. Jesus was into healing, feeding, forgiving, disturbing and washing feet. At the humblest level he was into management; into the business of setting other people free, free to be truly human. It was very personal but with astonishing social and political consequences, the most immediate of which was his own judicial execution.

That could all too easily lead to a cult of failure. A kind of spiritual inverse snobbery. Failure is not a proof of God's approval either. Even so, it was a perceptive Christian who said to me, speaking of a certain highly successful suburban congregation: 'It would take a saint of a vicar to empty that church.'

There is only one recorded sermon of Jesus in the New Testament, and that only in barest outline. Not, of course, the 'Sermon on the Mount' which is a collection of his most characteristic sayings. Jesus was on a visit to his home town, Nazareth. There, in the synagogue, he expounded a text from Isaiah which was about liberating captives, opening the eyes of the blind and setting the world's broken victims free. The central message of the sermon seemed to be that there were people outside the household of the true faith who understood that text better than many an Israelite and were, in consequence, rather closer to the Father. Irate, the congregation chased Jesus out of the synagogue and tried to kill him. The killing came a little later, with due respect for law and order. Habits have changed. British Christians this side of the Irish Channel would not do that kind of thing to a preacher. They would quietly stay away. But many Irish Christians would have a lot more sympathy with that Nazareth congregation. When one Presbyterian minister took the New Testament at its word and crossed the road to wish the Catholic priest a happy Christmas his congregation made life hell for him. He found refuge in England.

It is seldom realised just how offensive to the faithful Jesus must have been. To escape the offence now, many of his teachings have had their teeth drawn. Ask most people today what the best known of all the parables is about, and they will say to you: 'caring for those who have been mugged and robbed, being compassionate.' No Jew would need to be told something so basic. That the priest and the levite in the story were not decent Jews was offensive enough. But that was not the main point. In answer to the question: 'who is my neighbour?', Jesus comes up with the reply: 'the traditional enemy, the heretic, the Samaritan.' The villain turns out to be the hero, the good man. 'So,' says Jesus, 'go and be like him.' Is it any wonder that this young upstart of a preacher didn't get very far?

For all the eternal, cosmic significance of Calvary, its down-to-earth cause was the clash between the love of power and the power of love. The outcome of that struggle was then, and is now, creative suffering. The world calls it failure. That is why the reflections that follow will be very largely about failure, God's and ours.

I am not haunted by the martyrs of past and present. They give me hope. I am haunted by those who, loving power and wanting it for the Church, use the cross to inflict suffering, persecution and death on others. All too often I am their witting or unwitting accomplice. To challenge them can be costly.

Take apartheid. My awareness of this heresy dates back to the early sixties. I was a young curate in London's East End. Father Huddleston had just been ordered out of South Africa by his Community. At Sharpville women and men, peacefully demonstrating, had been shot down – in the back. All that, to maintain 'Christian civilisation'. Bishop Ambrose Reeves, the white Tutu of a generation ago, collected the evidence and told the world and was expelled.

In the *New Statesman* Vicky published a cartoon which has hung on my wall ever since to remind me of a truth that is not just about South Africa. A suffering face, black – but it need not have been – imposed on a cross in the shape of a swastika, the cross that signifies the power of the strong over the weak. Hitler's cross. As so often, Hitler was right. He knew, as many German Christians did not, that the true cross is subversive of power. Beside the suffering head on the cross, Vicky places this quotation from a speech by the then South African Prime Minister, Dr Verwoerd: 'We intend to do what is just and right as a Christian nation . . .' Under it all the words of Jesus: ' . . . for they know not what they do'.

Vicky was a Jew. He was brought up in Berlin and fled from Hitler with the secular ideals of a young socialist. He never lost them, and became the greatest of Britain's post-war cartoonists. He allowed his soul to cry as, day by day, he made others laugh. He made no claim to be a Christian but he had taken up his cross and followed the Jewish Man of Sorrows. When a British Labour government showed no sign of caring about the agony of Vietnam and its napalmed children, but caring a lot for its special relationship with rich America, he could carry the cross no longer and took his own life. The textbooks of moral theology tell us that suicide is a mortal sin. I shall let Vicky be my secular patron saint as I reflect on the cross in our world, the cross that takes on terrifying reality when one opens the files of Amnesty International's campaign against torture, the cross that the rich go on inflicting on the powerless and the poor, and – if not so obviously – the godly on a sceptical world.

But this will not be a catalogue of horror. Our mass media provide enough of that. It will rather be a reflection on experiences in a privileged life and richly varied ministry that has taken me to many corners of the earth. If the 'pedestrian' role of a parish priest for thirteen years in south-east London and of a British Council of Churches bureaucrat for a decade on the fringe of Belgravia is hardly reflected in these pages, it is not because ordinary things are boring and frustrating. They have as often been the source of joy and hope as of exasperation. I have chosen to share the less ordinary events in much the same way that my parishioners came to expect of me. Such experiences are unique only in the sense that every human experience is unique.

If, with John Wesley, I have been able to say and to feel that the world is my parish, let that not obscure the parallel truth that all the treasures and the terrors of the world are to be found in every parish and, in the end, in every human soul. If it is important to be aware of our global village, it is even more important to be aware that in every child in every village there is hidden the infinite love of God, a whole universe. So may each of these stories, each of these fragments of life, reveal something of the holiness of persons and the politics of love and never obscure that every human story has these divine ingredients.

2

Manhattan Penthouse

Vietnam was my door to America, a war that a great power, in the end, had the wisdom to lose. In the mid sixties the worst of the war was yet to come. The ecumenical movement was deeply troubled and sought, in every way possible, to support those American Christians who opposed the war. I was an Assistant Secretary in the International Affairs Department of the British Council of Churches and was responsible for East-West Relations. 'Please take on America as well' I was told one morning. So I did. America really meant Vietnam.

A lecture tour to pay for an American journey was quickly arranged. And a conference on the future of Indo-China thrown in. For me it was a voyage of discovery, a journey in search of America. It started in Manhattan, in midsummer. Not even Singapore had seemed as humid and hot. On Seventh Avenue, two blocks from the United Nations Building, the Episcopal Church – American Anglicanism – has its head-quarters. In its penthouse a guest-room had been reserved for me. My colleague in the office below who had made all my American arrangements put me in the elevator and assured me I'd be most warmly welcomed by the hostess at the top. My sexist – I didn't know the word then – apprehensions were quickly proved groundless. A large, warm and motherly black woman, straight out of American colonial fiction, took me to her heart. She had a great problem. The previous guest in the room booked for me had decided to stay a night longer. Would I make the sacrifice of sharing with him. 'Of course,' I said. 'It's no sacrifice at all.' Much relieved, she knocked on the door and sent me in. The other guest had already agreed to my coming.

In stylish pyjamas he was sitting in bed, reading. He stretched out his hand and told me his name. I told him mine. (Had this been England, we might never have known.) His great American handshake said: 'It sure is a unique honour and pleasure to meet with you.' It felt genuine, even though he must have wished I was coming a day later. He resumed reading and I started unpacking my much plainer pyjamas. (It wasn't until later in the permissive sixties that I learnt to travel lighter, without them.) Having showered, in a country where showers really work, I was ready to occupy the other bed. Before that, it seemed right to do what my companion had obviously done, to hang my clothes in the rosewood wardrobe.

I was faced with a beautifully tailored blue dress-uniform, heavy with brass. Among the stars and other insignia there was a cross. And another on the other side of the jacket. My room-mate was evidently a high ranking military chaplain. As it turned out, the Deputy Chaplain General of the United States Air Force. And a fellow Anglican priest. I had last worn a uniform at high school as Sergeant-Major of the cadet corps. When it came to my call up for military service I registered as a conscientious objector and have been a Christian pacifist ever since. My room-mate was presumably right at the other end of the moral spectrum, convinced that in Vietnam and elsewhere there was only one way to deal with 'godless communism'. Yet I was the guest of Americans who believed that this war was at best a tragic mistake, at worst a horrific crime.

My father had the kind of faith that made him sure there was no such thing as pure chance. Occasions like this first night in America made me feel he must be right. I was determined not to waste it. Given the more than cordial greeting, my companion seemed strangely uninterested in my presence. Once I was sitting in bed like him, however, I made him put down his book by explaining what had brought me to America and, without further small-talk, asking him to help me understand his role in the war. 'How do you relate to the bomber crews, sent to "take out" whole Vietcong villages?'

I expected one of two alternatives. Either, and most probably, a view of this war as a crusade against communism, a simple issue of a Christian struggle against a pagan foe; and therefore no problem for a military chaplain. Or else a much more sophisticated answer, some version of the just war doctrine, seeing this war, like all others, as tragic evidence of human failure, trying to keep it as humane as possible, maintaining a chaplaincy service that would help those in the battle not to dehumanise the enemy, being a light – the light of Christ – in the midst of darkness.

None of that. Though he must have been aware that there was a great moral conflict raging in America over this war, he showed no sign of it. The rights and wrongs of the war were not his concern. He was employed as a priest by the US government to do what he could to help maintain the morale of the US Air Force and that was largely seen in terms of helping the young men to steer clear of illicit sex and drugs. Had he been of more evangelical persuasion he would no doubt and, more importantly, have been able to offer personal salvation to the unconverted as well. His role was purely pastoral. He was in no position to make any judgement about the rights and wrongs of the war. That is what governments are for. If they are wrong, they must answer for it.

We did not converse for long. I hope he slept, after that, better than I did. I should not have been so surprised or shattered by my fellow priest's response. I knew, but did not want to admit to myself, what worlds can separate Christians within the same Church, priests within the same Communion. Between this man and me there was a great spiritual chasm. He, I had to remind myself, represented – in an unthinking kind of way – the position held through many centuries by most Christians, the separation of pastoral care from any understanding of the whole world as potentially God's Kingdom, of a cosmic struggle going on in every society and in every soul between the Inner Light and the Prince of Darkness.

Worlds separated me from my companion. We were strangers in the night. I cannot tell whether he shared some of my pain, made greater because he was as likeable as most cultured Americans. My pain was not really about him at all. I did not know him as a human being. Any more than he knew me. We parted in the morning in the most friendly way. No one would have guessed at any alienation between us. It was the cross on his uniform that had kept us apart, the cross worn not as a sign of contradiction to the world of power but as a captive to that world, trapped among the military insignia.

It did not take me long to realise that this encounter could have happened almost anywhere in the western world. There was nothing particularly American about it. Chaplains had served in Hitler's armies on precisely these terms. They were doing no more than giving Caesar what is due to him – and no doubt often with courage and deep dedication, sharing suffering and death. I should have remembered that prayers were said for the crew by a chaplain before they set off for Hiroshima. I should have remembered that Gordon Zahn's sociological study of the Royal Air Force Chaplaincy in Britain revealed that most British chaplains would have answered my questions just as their American colleague did.

I should have remembered too that in Soviet Russia, after years of bitter persecution of the Russian Orthodox Church, Stalin, during World War II, turned to a revived Church to back up the war effort with fervent patriotism. Young Soviet Christians serve today in the Red Army with their Church's full support. A chaplaincy would gladly be provided, if only an atheist government did not rule it out.

In short, I should have known – and did know – that the cross at the heart of the Church is an unresolved struggle between those who see the Church as a chaplaincy, a kind of service agency, to the world and its institutions and those who see the Church, the Body of Christ, as a radical alternative to those institutions.

The answer almost certainly does not lie in choosing one of these alternatives and declaring the other to be heretical. It lies in living with the sometimes almost unbearable tension between them, between two strands in the New Testament and in the tradition of the Church. If 'God so loved the world . . .' then he did not send his son to be at war with it. Yet because he was at war with its depravity, he became its victim.

Had I asked him, my companion that first night in Manhattan would no doubt have expressed admiration for Martin Luther King, though I can't be sure. It was not until his death that he became an object of almost universal acclaim. It was Dr King who, in one of his sermons, had said that it is not the task of the Church to be subservient to the state or to be its master, but to be its conscience. That is a creative and costly form of service. It prays for and respects the principalities and powers of this world but is not their spiritual strong arm. It lives in critical solidarity with the whole human family in all its social and political structures. And the Churches themselves belong in that world of structures, not significantly better or worse than the world of which they are part.

That is perhaps the most difficult thing of all for Christians to grasp. The uniqueness of the gospel does not make those who believe it unique in wisdom, in goodness or in the power to change what is to what should be. The Christian critique of the world does not stem from a position of moral or spiritual superiority but of shared responsibility and shared guilt. What is unique to those with faith, however fragile that faith may be, is an awareness of the divine mercy and of a God who shares the brokenness of the world, who is put to death in the world and who, beyond and through death, is the assurance of life. When everything else has lost meaning, God, dimly perceived by us as love in human form, is all the meaning, eternal meaning, that we need.

If it is true that critical solidarity with ourselves and with all human phenomena characterises the life of the Church at its best (because it also describes God's relationship with us) then clearly there remains a vast area of potential disagreement as to what that means in day-to-day practice. Once the tension is accepted, here is the area of creative dialogue within the

Church. The traditional denominational and confessional divisions within the Church are totally irrelevant to this tension. Arguably they are an anachronism and an irrelevance which – if they cannot be negotiated away – must simply be overridden. They are an impediment to dealing with life's true agenda, with God's real world.

Two significant things separated me from the man in the smart pyjamas. One was much more serious than the other. The serious one was my conviction that the Christian life means to live with profound contradictions and that these go to the heart of the faith and are symbolised by the Son of Man dying on a cross. The crucifixion itself, if it is the centrepiece of salvation history, puts a major question mark against the fundamental concept of a loving Father. If Abraham did not, in the end, have to kill Isaac, why must the bloody spectacle on Calvary, and all the world's other calvaries, be played out to the end? The man who does not see the problem of the cross on his uniform, does not see the problem of the cross.

Our less important difference is the more obvious one. The chaplain is clearly not a Christian pacifist, and I am. My option for pacifism, not as a dogma or even as a moral absolute, but as an attempt to combat evil in a Christian way, does not solve a whole range of problems. The theology of the New Testament and the witness of the early Church make it much easier to be a pacifist than not to be, but in the end my reasoning is simpler and does not depend on great learning: I cannot both love my enemy and be prepared – as war demands – to kill my enemy. There must always be some alternative if St Paul is right in asking the Church in Rome not to let itself be overcome by evil, but to defeat evil with goodness.

But given a fallen world and great evil which, apparently, cannot be overcome peacefully, it is not surprising that the demanding ethic of Mahatma Gandhi does not command the consent of most Christians. I am almost as disturbed by my fellow pacifists who lightly or even scornfully dismiss the doctrine of the just war, as I am by the military chaplain who cannot recognise the contradiction he represents.

The case for the just war is not hard to make – in theory. The tragedy of the Church has generally, however, been that it has ignored its own rules, its own carefully weighed ethical criteria, and has simply assumed that 'our war' must be just. More often than not, both sides have made that assumption: an evident nonsense. Considering both cause and conduct together, very few wars have in fact been 'just', as defined by the theologians. As, in the nuclear age, no war between major nations could be or remain just, the whole question poses itself in a new way. The ethical debate becomes very largely a weighing up of how war can best be prevented.

Yet that was not the issue which was – during this visit to America – tearing the nation apart. Impressively, as few other nations ever have, and as few Churches have helped their nation to do, Americans were facing the question of how to get out of an unjust war. In that context my first place of pilgrimage was to the house of the *Catholic Worker*. Here, among the unemployed, the junkies, the poorest of New York's poor Dorothy Day and her friends had kept open house since the Depression of the thirties. For many years the community's newspaper had, month by month, been living evidence for me of the kind of worldly sanctity that St Francis had stood for. Its cover price of one cent has never been increased.

Worlds separated 'my' penthouse from Dorothy Day's welcoming soup kitchen where there were no barriers at all, where university professors and the most derelict of characters were treated with equal dignity. Here there was no need to debate Vietnam. On the night I came, the talk was of how, through prayer and action, Americans might help to end apartheid in South Africa. Not until twenty years later did most American Christians even begin to think that had anything to do with them.

And here I first learnt about the remarkable Berrigan brothers. Within a short time Daniel, poet, politician, teacher, clown and Jesuit, was to become my friend. His simple yet demanding openness made friendship both easy and costly. Not from him the all-American handshake but the immediate question: 'Brother, will you come on pilgrimage with us?' That pilgrimage might have ended anywhere; for Dan and many of his friends it often passed through some prison or other. His 'Notes from the Underground and letters from Danbury Prison' (no, he didn't choose it to match his name!) were published as *America is Hard to Find*. Compared to many other places, given its remarkable openness, I found America – and not just one America – remarkably easy to find and very hard not to love, as well as to hate.

My conference was to be near Washington DC. 'See you there then!' Dan said compellingly. He told me the exact time and place. Anything but a hideout for dissidents or a place of welcome for the poor. One of Washington's smartest hotels. Here Daniel was to receive from the Catholic Sodalities of America the Pope John XXIII Peace Prize. To what other American Catholic could such a prize be given, even by such a conservative body of American Catholics?

It was a glittering occasion of Washington Catholic high society. Yes, a place had been reserved for me at the celebration dinner. But, at the hour appointed, Father Daniel and his party from New York had not arrived. When, dramatically, they did, the contrast between those waiting and those arriving could not have been greater. In an old clapped out bus Dan and with him the poor America, the alternative America, came on the scene. It was chaplinesque farce. Which means it was dead serious.

A correctly dressed bishop presided in the way, I presume, one does at such dinners. With charm, some humour and genteel grace. Father Dan, by now, sat next to him at a very high high-table. He was invited, dressed (unless my memory badly deceives me) anything but correctly, to give the 'address of honour'. It was pure poetry, though in prose. My antennae only picked up fragments of meaning. For the presiding bishop there was the backhanded reassurance that in the divine dispensation there was a place, even for people dressed in various shades of purple. For them, the humble task of oiling the ecclesiastical machinery, leaving others free – if they had the courage – to *be* the Church. And a lot more, with tongue in cheek, in that vein. For many of those present the spiritual distance from the speaker must have been too great to make it possible to listen or, at any rate, to hear. A little bit like Jesus in his home-town synagogue. I started feeling sorry for the presiding bishop. So, I think, did the bishop. When it came to presenting the prize he did it, though the humour and the grace were by now more strained. The real and ultimate moment of truth did not come until the very end. The bishop concluded (how else?) by announcing that it was his duty to convey to those present the blessing of the Holy Father. But should he really? In the light of all he had heard and half understood, was it fitting? He did not know. So – hedging his bets, playing it safe – he announced to the assembled company: 'I convey to you the blessing of the Holy Father – conditionally.'

I did not see Daniel's face. At any rate he did not laugh aloud. And God's laughter mixed with God's tears was not flashed up on a large screen. Celestial Videos Inc. had not yet been thought of. This was the stuff of real Church history when a spiritual force meets an ecclesiastical system and normal communication breaks down.

I had found very important fragments of America, fragments of a living mosaic. Far from that story leading me to cynicism about the Catholic hierarchy or American society, I know today that, over the years that followed, real spiritual encounters did happen; even, I suspect, that night. Were it not so the Catholic Bishops' Conference would hardly have been able to produce its prophetic pastoral letter on nuclear weapons and another on the moral implications of the American economic system.

It matters little whether, as in the United States, there is a formal separation of religious institutions from the state or as in England and some other parts of western Europe the old patterns of established religion still survive: in practice the Churches almost everywhere have to make their voice heard as best they can in healthy competition with others. The temptation to 'lord it' over society has virtually gone. In that secular context the task of Church leadership is highly complex, yet filled with creative opportunity. The great temptation is to hold compulsively to the middle ground while remaining in dialogue both with radical base groups and with a stolid conservative membership. Jesus, of course, would not by any stretch of the imagination have qualified as a 'moderate' in first-century Jerusalem. Moderates don't get arrested, tortured, tried and executed. Not normally, anyway. What Daniel Berrigan helped me to understand better is that only exceptionally will religious leaders be expected to play the Jesus role. That really is for the people who are mature enough and immature enough to be clown, court jester and fool for Christ's sake. When, rarely, high office and high risk-taking go hand-in-hand – as in Tutu's South Africa – it is almost time to speak of miracles.

In fact such wonders keep happening. The Holy Spirit cannot be programmed. It took a cautious, circumspect Archbishop of Canterbury who usually sees all twelve sides of every issue to shake a spiritually dormant British establishment which was taking inordinate pride in military victory, by preaching a 'victory' sermon which put national chauvinism firmly in its place, and penitence and compassion gently, yet with authority, at the centre.

It was about two years after the Washington ceremony that I met Daniel Berrigan again, now a chaplain at Cornell University. Verbal opposition to the war had turned to symbolic acts of civil disobedience. Within weeks Daniel went 'underground' and then, at a time of his own choosing, to jail. Both while on the run, preaching and teaching as he went, and later locked up with his priest brother Philip, he wrote some of the most important spiritual counsel to come out of America in recent times, none of it more perceptive than a letter to his fellow Jesuits about discipleship today; his letter, which I summarise, is dated 10 April 1970:

This week marks the anniversary of the deaths of Dietrich Bonhoeffer (1945) and Teilhard de Chardin (1955). It is the week that we, the felons of Catonsville, are summoned by the state to begin our prison sentence. No one of us needs to be told that the times are such as to bring despair to all but the strongest. My own hope at this point remains firm. I hope that at least a minority of us Jesuits may remain together in the years ahead to form a confessing brotherhood, a community in which men speak the truth to men, in which our lives may be purified of the inhuman drives of egoism, cultural conformity, professional pride and dread of life. A brotherhood which will be skilled in a simple, all but lost art – the reading of the gospel, and life according to its faith.

Many of our Church leaders are effectively innoculated against Christ and his Spirit. Nothing is to be expected from such men, except the increasing suffocation of the Word. But the real question is not the conversion of cardinals or presidents, but the conversion of each of us.

Most of us are obsessed with the inevitability of change. We talk persuasively of it, we grasp at new forms and styles. And yet the suspicion remains; very few of us have the courage to measure our passion for moral change against the sacrifice of what lies closest to our hearts: our good name, our comfort, our security, our professional status.

And yet until such things are placed at risk, nothing changes. The gospel says it. So do the times. Unless the cries of the war victims, the disenfranchised, the prisoners, the hopeless poor, the resisters of conscience – unless the cry of the world reaches our ears and we measure our lives and deaths against those of others, nothing changes. Least of all ourselves; we stand like sticks and stones, impervious to the meaning of history or the cry of its Lord and Victim.

To me, ever since, this has been more than a passionate tract for the times but a confession of faith against which, frighteningly, to measure my own life. Daniel signed off: 'I ask your prayers, that my brother and I, and all who are at the edge, may be found faithful and obedient; in good humour, and always at your side. Daniel Berrigan SJ.' Then, still in hiding, he began to write his most remarkable prose-poem, *The Passion of Dietrich Bonhoeffer*.

3

The Special Licence

Late in the sixties, the last decade that London still felt close
to the centre of the universe, John Robinson, Bishop of Wool-
wich, who with *Honest to God* had so disturbed a complacent
Church of England, offered me a job in his corner of London.
He had persuaded the small band of the faithful at the Church
of the Ascension, Blackheath, to let me come as their vicar,
with a package of other tasks thrown in. Dartmouth Row,
originally built in the late seventeenth century by the Earl of
Dartmouth to house officers of the Naval Academy in Greenwich, was still *that* kind of street; the Church in its original
1697 form had been the Earl's private chapel. Christopher
Wren probably designed it. The only parishioner I already
knew was the mildly iconoclastic Tory writer John Grigg who,
as Lord Altrincham (a title he later renounced) had mildly
criticised the Royal household and upset a good many people
in and outside Fleet Street.

But most of the people who lived in this small parish were
inhabitants of two of the GLC's poorest estates. Top people
(the editor of *The Times* had just moved out) lived close to the
poorest – and they never met. There were not many 'ordinary'
in-between church-goers. Freedom was the watchword of the
bishop's sermon at my colourful, ecumenical institution. I was
charged with relating the 'glorious liberty of the children of
God' to a local Church of England parish in south-east London.
My predecessor had been a strict play-it-by-the-rules legalistic
churchman. The naval tradition still hung around. I'd always
liked seamen. I was reminded that in nearby Deptford Peter
the Great of Russia had once learnt to build ships. Greenwich

was heavy with naval history; the professor of the subject was to be our neighbour.

I came with no blueprint. But with the conviction that openness to God and to the world should characterise the life of the parish through the decade for which I had decided to stay. That, for me, my wife and our four children, turned into thirteen rewarding, unpredictable years. Sydney Carter composed and sang a song for my institution about the impossibility of locking up the Holy Spirit in any church:

Bird of Heaven

Catch the Bird of Heaven, lock him in a cage of gold
Look again tomorrow and he will be gone.

Ah the Bird of Heaven! Follow where the Bird has gone
If you want to find him, keep on travelling on.

Lock him in religion. Gold and frankincense and myrrh
Carry to his prison, but he will be gone.

Temple made of marble, beak and feather made of gold
Bell and book and candle, but he will be gone.

Bell and book and candle cannot hold him any more
Still the Bird is flying, as he did before.

Ah the Bird of Heaven! Follow where the Bird has gone
If you want to find him, keep on travelling on.

It was not too difficult to persuade the parish council to keep the central door of the church, at pavement level, permanently open, its wooden panels replaced by plate glass and the sanctuary lit all night. The word soon spread. Specially in the winter. It became a temporary home for many and for Albert, the 'resident tramp', for seven years. At the end of thirteen years I was able to assure the sceptics and the fearful that nothing worse than stolen candlesticks and (very occasional) shit in the pulpit had befallen this beautiful house of God.

Of course there was a price to pay for us in the vicarage opposite. Lore, my wife, did most of the paying. Being there for all the human problems that drifted into Dartmouth Row. Yet many a winter night, I slept with an uneasy conscience in our grand Victorian vicarage. 'God's house' was open to all, our own was closed to all but a few. The really open Church . . . the open hearts and hands and homes of the people of God was little more than a far-off vision. The credibility gap remained enormous between the gospel we preached and the life we lived. If our congregation in its search to make God's openness real was at least aware that we could only survive as forgiven sinners, that was a beginning on which we could build.

The first serious challenge to my new policy of openness, of gospel before law, came within our first week. A ring on the door bell very late at night. 'May I come in?' John was a civil servant who lived around the corner. Not a churchgoer. We had not met before. 'Vicar, will you please marry us, tomorrow, if possible? My divorce has just come through. I'm free to marry now and my fiancée is in hospital with terminal cancer. This will fulfil her last wish.'

The complexities of Church and State law on marriage were a book of seven seals to me. I had no idea of what I was or was not entitled to do. I promised to find out the next morning. In my heart I had no doubt what I should do.

This much I did know: the clergy were under instruction not to agree to the remarriage of the divorced in Church. Surely, I said to myself, that could not apply in such a case. I was wrong and on collision course with the law, or rather with the Church's interpretation of the law. The law of the land would have permitted me to marry this couple in my church. I was entitled to ignore the ecclesiastical instruction not to do so. But a wedding in hospital was, legally, quite a different matter. Only by special licence of the Archbishop of Canterbury (regardless of the couple's religion or lack of it) could a wedding be conducted outside a place licensed for that purpose.

So, to the Archbishop's legal officer in the hope of this special licence. The answer was no. The Archbishop cannot issue it to a divorced person whose former partner is still alive. 'Cannot or will not?' I asked. He did, it emerged, have discretion to do whatever he thought right, but in view of the Church's teaching on marriage his position was clear. I insisted that he must personally decide. He was on holiday. The matter was put to him; how, I could not discover. The answer was still no. An individual priest might exercise his discretion, but the Archbishop could not ignore the rules he issues to others. I had come to a full stop. No way could I legally marry this couple. Was there no way to achieve the same end by civil law? A registrar's wedding which I could then bless? Not that either. The law had been unchanged since the middle ages. The Church had done nothing to surrender this monopoly strictly administered by the Archbishop's legal officer.

I went back to John and told him the awful truth. But I had already made up my mind to go ahead, regardless. My compassion as a human being and my duty as a priest were quite clear to me. To that I added my sense of justice. The law was worse than an ass. It was a denial of justice. This couple, had they both been healthy, could have married at any time in a registrar's office or, if I agreed, in my church.

The law might obstruct both mercy and justice. I would not. So (it was now the third day) I informed my bishop, who ventured no opinion but simply – and rightly – told me I must follow my conscience.

In Higher Green hospital, with nurses as witnesses, the marriage took place. A last wish had been fulfilled. The wife did not live a day longer. In God's eyes, in mine, in the bride's and groom's this was a real marriage. But I knew, in law the bride still died a single woman. Her husband appealed to the Registrar of Births, Deaths and Marriages. When he heard the facts he simply ruled that, whatever the letter of the law might say, he would register this as the death of a married woman. At least after death the State showed mercy where before death the Church had not.

That experience etched itself deeply on my subsequent ministry. It was an important but very significant sign to me what deadly legalism the Churches have imposed on human beings through many centuries. In the maintenance of a theoretical principle, the sanctity of the marriage vows in this case, love of human beings had been sacrificed. I had been taught a lesson. I had learnt in a practical way how easy it is for the Church to inflict the cross on the world rather than to help carry the world's crosses.

The marriage performed and, in this case, the dead buried, was not the end of this story. For it illustrates the close relationship between persons and politics, between human needs and aspirations, and the law's capacity to meet or to frustrate those needs. The next pastoral step was to get the law changed so that no priest would again be faced with my dilemma.

I made known widely what had happened among those who could do something about it, members of parliament. A private member's bill, I felt, was the way ahead, a bill giving the Registrar General powers hitherto held only by the Church. And that is what happened. An MP on the far right of the Tory party who had had his share of marital traumas readily saw the point and did what was needed. It gave me pleasure to be working on this with someone with whom, in most other contexts, I would find myself at loggerheads.

To get reform in the State was a lot easier than to move the Church. Part of the frustration of belonging to the Church of England's General Synod, its parliament, is to have sat through days and weeks of debate, over several years, on the re-ordering of the Church's marriage rules. Learned report after learned report has suggested reforms. They have all come to nothing. In essence the debate has turned almost solely on whether a person, once married in church, can marry a new partner there, if the earlier marriage has failed. No, say the rigorists. That would devalue the marriage vows made the first time. Let them be married by the State and let the priest then bless that marriage, if he is so minded. That ignores, of course, that in the marriage contract neither the Church nor the State marries a couple. They marry each other. Their vows, regardless of where they are made, are of fundamental importance. To that, the Church can then add its blessing and the State its authority.

For the Church to refuse to 'marry' but then to bless is a nonsense. But far worse, to discriminate against second marriages (which may be much more profoundly serious than the first) is to deny the most fundamental thing about the Christian faith: that in all things and at all times we are forgiven sinners, always making a new start. Always, except in marriage? Is a failed marriage *the* unforgivable sin? No one seriously thinks it is. Yet for some desired social or even spiritual good, the Church must go on denying the doctrine of God's free grace.

In fact, of course, it is not quite like that at all any more. While the hard-line rule stands, most bishops now allow or encourage their clergy to follow their conscience. Now what can and cannot be done depends in what parish you happen to live. A reversal of gospel realities. Strict law, liberally administered, being paramount, instead of the principle of freedom with certain guidelines to give it shape and structure and even discipline. Canon lawyers have a lot to answer for but the shame is not theirs. The Churches appoint them and instruct them on the type of cages they are to build for the Bird of Heaven. And of course – again and again – it escapes. There is room in all the Churches for those who keep opening the cage's door. Those who, in their frustration, leave their Church behind for another or even start another will often find an even more secure cage. Or a desert with no living water. To be engaged in the struggle between law and gospel is part of what it means to be human. But to seek to live wholly without restraints is as utopian in the spiritual as in the secular world.

Of course our church's ever open door meant a slightly higher insurance premium. It took the police a good many years to learn that the light had not been left on and the church left open at two in the morning by accident. A knock at that hour was usually from a stopping patrol car. There were many other encounters, good and bad, with the police. Some deserve lengthy treatment in their own right. One principle seemed to me almost sacrosanct. I would never turn anyone who had taken refuge in our church over to the police. I was to learn that genuine openness to human need throws doubt even on such a good principle. Though in fact I never did break it, there were times when I felt that a spell in prison might have been the best of all the options.

Malcolm, as I suspected, was something like the church's semi-resident thief and, on the whole, happier inside than outside prison. That, at any rate, is where he was relaxed and capable of reasonably sustained conversation. The evidence that he had made off with the candlesticks and the processional cross was overwhelming. The candlesticks quickly went to earth in the trade. But who will buy a nicked cross? Malcolm just couldn't get rid of it. So he threw it into the Thames at high tide. At the next low tide a boatman saw it and took it to the local police. It was back with us within twenty-four hours. Malcolm's face as I walked in with it gave him away. From that day on, he was sure crosses have magic powers. I could assure him, they haven't. Not ornamental ones, made of brass. The Church could as well do without them.

The cross that some of us did bear was living with our own failure and that of the community around us to provide an environment for Malcolm and others like him to live satisfying lives outside prison. A much more basic failure, shared by almost all our Churches, is our cultural isolation from those many who live at the edge or beyond it, who live and yet barely live and to whom our liturgies are as irrelevant as the rest of our lives. These liturgies presuppose that we are – in St Paul's words – 'one new humanity' in Christ. How can that ikon of truth, that image, be turned into reality? If the social derelicts are in some special way loved by God, how do we honour Christ in them? Christ in Roy as, in frustrated anger, he smashes another empty bottle on the vicarage steps?

Theological college had not even taught me how to pray about that, let alone what to do about it, or how to help my wife cope with it. My sermons about the Kingdom seemed strangely irrelevant to so much of the real world which came in through our open door. It may not seem much, nor is it an answer to the Church of England's shameful rejection of the ministry of women: but I believe that the endless cups of coffee served to the needy and not so needy by my wife at our door were sacraments of Holy Communion. No less. Because of them and their many equivalents in the lives of others, we could dare to meet each Sunday morning, break bread and celebrate Eucharist. And we could say boldly, despite our doubts and fears: 'The Lord is here.'

4

Suliman

My encounters with power started early, even if I don't count
the time when German army officers took away our BMW. It
was needed, they said, for the *Anschluss*, the invasion of
Austria, and a Jewish doctor had no business to be driving
around in it anyway. They didn't say the last bit. We just
assumed that's what they must have thought. It actually came
back, filthy, hardly recognisable, but in time to use it to flee
from the Gestapo to Berlin. It was easier to hide in the big city
while struggling to get permission to emigrate to somewhere;
anywhere where they'd let us in.

Very distant relatives, not Jews, agreed to let me stay in
their basement flat. Infinitely kind people, willing to take risks.
To me it was an adventure, better than being in school.
Occasionally I'd see my mother. My parents tried never to
sleep more than two nights in one place.

It was something special for my mother to take me out for
a walk. It was on 9 November 1938. I remember the big shops
and the colourful window displays. It was all so much grander
and more impressive than in our little country town. Berlin has
always been worth a visit. But my mother grew tense. Lorries
stopped at intervals by the roadside, filled with black uniformed
men. A whistle blew and they jumped down and were suddenly
all round us, swinging great truncheons and smashing up the
shop fronts. Sudden terror and broken glass all round us.
Jewish shops. We got away quickly, physically unharmed. My
mother wasn't Jewish, only my father. And I didn't look
Jewish. But the damage had been done. It was the day the
great Nazi pogroms began in earnest. The day the synagogues

throughout Germany were set alight. Though my parents had tried to shelter me from the truth, I knew in my bones, this was not about *them*, it was about *us*.

Never again could I readily assume that those in power, those in uniform, those who made the decisions about others were on the side of justice, or even of the law. I learnt quickly that for some people life is very dangerous . . . and it's no good appealing to the police. The police were the danger.

But my mother taught me early never, like the Nazis, to hate whole groups of people. She reminded me that her father, the grandfather we'd had to leave behind, had been a policeman. I loved and respected him. For him, the child of poor peasants, with no land to inherit, a career in the police force of the local duke had been quite something in the 1880s. And because grandfather was a good, conscientious policeman he finished up, much later, as the deputy governor of a model prison. But now he was unemployed. When Hitler's first political prisoners were brought to be locked up (they were probably communists and he was a staunch conservative) he took his keys, put them down on the governor's desk and resigned. He had served since the days of the Kaiser to maintain law and order. Locking men up who had broken no law was not his business. He was never to work again, and had his only son – to his grief – not been an influential Nazi, he might have fared a lot worse.

But had more men and women had the principles and courage of my grandfather, had more Germans stood up to Hitler's flouting of law and human decency, history might have taken a very different turn. Whatever some might do with their power over others, I had learnt not to make hasty judgements. And had some of my grandfather's principles not also become mine, I might never have finished up so totally committed to the work of Amnesty International.

If the broken glass of November 1938 was my first conscious trauma, the second, a few months later, took on much greater significance. By early 1939 we were among the lucky ones. New Zealand had said yes to us. With all our papers in order, we could actually leave Germany like normal travellers. Or almost so. There was a regulation for every category of Jew. My father had fought for Germany in World War I and had won the Iron Cross First Class. Our money was forfeit to the German state. But we could take our possessions with us to our country of destination and pay for the passage ourselves from our bank account which, for every other purpose, had been blocked. So, with characteristic cheek, my father booked the most expensive passage possible to New Zealand. That much money anyway he would take out of Hitler's coffers. It was within the letter of the law.

It nearly all came unstuck. The New Zealand government insisted that even refugees must land with at least £100 sterling each. In 1939 that was a lot of money, specially if you had none at all. We needed £300 in a hurry . . . much more like £3000 today. We phoned a distant relative in Shanghai. Could he help? No. But he knew a Frenchman who just might, and gave us his phone number. Jean Carette, mayor of Rieux, Oise. My father rang him, told him our story and without a moment's hesitation he simply said: 'It will be an honour to help you. Where shall I send the money?' 'To Amsterdam,' my father said. And he sent it, in US dollars, without the slightest guarantee that he would ever see a penny of it again. To such people, as World War II drew near, many Jews owed their lives. But because there were not more of them and because most countries had closed their doors to more Jewish refugees, many who might have been saved went to the gas-chambers.

So we left Berlin, the letter J for Jew stamped on each page of our Nazi passports, valid for one journey out of the Reich. Exile was bitter for my parents. Culturally, come what may, they would always remain Germans. They would never allow Bach and Goethe to be smeared with the fascist brush. The journey to Amsterdam was made in tears.

But for me it was yet one more exciting adventure. We were travelling state class on the luxury liner *Johan van Oldenbarnevelt*. I, all of seven years old, was game for anything, so I thought. In fact I provided some drama right away. My parents, and many others, stood on deck at the railing watching Europe slowly recede. A time for painful parting. And for me a time to explore. Not far away I discovered one of the great water hydrants. What would happen, I wondered, if I turned it on? With all my strength I wrenched at it, it turned and a great rush of water flooded the deck, dowsing a lot of the people. When my parents discovered who the culprit was, they lost any doubts they might have had about corporal punishment. The next morning, a knock on their door. A steward with a huge box of chocolates addressed: 'To the little boy who drowned all my sorrows.' I was learning that the consequences of one's actions can never be accurately predicted. Anyway, my sense of adventure had not been impaired.

Our fellow passengers in the exclusive part of the ship were rich Dutch planters returning to their estates in the East Indies and a member of the House of Lords and his family on a pleasure cruise. No children. Poor refugees in *that* company. The material for tragi-comedy. Charlie Chaplin could have made a lot of it.

For the first and last time in my life I had my own servant, my 'boy' as he was described. He was probably in his mid twenties, sitting, white-uniformed and turbaned, cross-legged outside my door, waiting for instructions. He was Javanese and his name was Suliman. Despite the language barrier, he quickly became my only real friend and played games with me. But not all the time, of course. Luxury, I quickly learnt, is very boring. So, I went exploring. I think I must have inherited my father's cheek and non-conformity. It was only fun to dare go where I knew I wasn't allowed to be.

I climbed down a steel ladder into the engine room and found the huge turbines greatly impressive. My courage had paid off. No one chased me away. Then came a further challenge. Another steel ladder. Down I went under the engines. It got darker and even hotter. Now I really was scared, but I pushed on to the very bottom of the liner, the only light from above dimly casting shadows. I was standing on straw-covered wooden planks. I took a step and my foot hit a body, lying asleep. I froze with fear and guilt and shame. At my feet was lying one of the Javanese boys and around him there were more. I had stumbled into the world where they slept when they were not working.

The poor little rich boy that I was, had discovered on the liner of dreams a fragment of reality. One day I would learn that this was called colonialism and exploitation. At that moment I only knew that I wanted to get back to the security of my parents as quickly as possible. Crying, I made my way back and remember nothing of that. Only what I had discovered.

It was a lot more shocking than Hitler's SS men smashing windows. It demolished my assumption that all human beings were, more or less, of equal value. Head on, I'd met privilege and oppression. I was privileged and my friend Suliman wasn't. It hurt very badly and it's only a process of self-protection that makes it hurt less now. The nightmare of the second ladder recurred for years. In fact now I can no longer tell what is memory of the event and what is memory of its nightmarish sequel. What is now clear is that the *Johan van Oldenbarnevelt* was a microcosm of our world.

I cannot put a date on my conversion to Christ, though it began in early childhood. I hope it is still happening. I can put a date on my conversion to the world. It was this traumatic experience of injustice. It has, ever since, shaped both what I am and what I have failed to be. It has made me fight the world as it is; as I discovered it then and as it has remained. And it has always left me dissatisfied with my own degree of commitment to the struggle. Without the other, much more mysterious, conversion to Christ I might often have despaired of myself and of the world's inhumanity.

It is all this, that made me want to study politics and, when I had graduated, say to myself that I would not really make sense of what I had learnt until I had also studied theology. So I did that and then learnt that faith, hope and love are not academic disciplines but fragments of life, perceived through failure and forgiveness.

The study of Marxism taught me that even good people are

helpless in the face of evil, unstoppable systems and that creative change is not possible without a common struggle. Life has taught me – and the gospel confirms it – that none of us are immune from the corruptions of power and that revolutionary justice without compassion is not always an improvement on the old oppression. All too often – for fear of something worse – Christians knowing this, have stood in the way of radical change and safeguarded their vested interests instead of bringing to the revolution itself the humanity of Christ, with all the attendant risks.

However personally significant for me, my luxury liner experience needs a political postscript. The world war that began so soon after my journey also brought with it an end to colonialism. Yet the Indonesia that had been set free from Dutch rule did not radically change and, after a bloody coup in its early history, became a State with perhaps more persecuted people and at any rate more prisoners of conscience than any other. It would be good to think that it was simply the wrong group who had come to power, the right instead of the left. Experience does not bear that out. I fear that all those with easy ideological answers have been and remain the great deceivers of our century.

Of course that does not mean that piety is to be preferred to politics. It is to the affirmation of politics that my conversion to the world has led me. Not, of course, to the exclusion of God the Holy Spirit, but as the natural consequence of a spirituality based on the Incarnation, the affirmation that God is to be found not only in Jesus but (because of who Jesus was) in every human being.

When the Russian mystic and political philosopher Nicholas Berdyaev wrote, early in this century, that 'bread for myself is a material question but bread for my neighbour is a spiritual question' he was, in effect, saying that what is behind every economic policy is a prior spiritual decision about who is entitled to what.

The present trading and financial policies of the industrial nations perpetuate the situation on the ocean liner. The haves dictate to the have-nots how things shall be. The moral – and therefore spiritual – priorities of those with power become even clearer when the military spending of the rich is set against what even a small fragment of this money could do to save the lives of the poorest. Our protection from a possible future foe is held to be infinitely more important than the defeat of present hunger. How great is the moral difference between killing people deliberately, for some supposedly good reason, as Hitler did with the mentally ill, and allowing people to die because Trident missiles, though vastly more expensive, are held to be better nuclear deterrents than Polaris missiles?

Using such an example may of course be moving into the field of moral surrealism. It is probable that any policy that embraces the possibility – or even, given the right circumstances, the certainty – of using weapons of mass destruction is spiritually bankrupt from the outset.

That does not make me despair of politics any more than I despair of people. The macro- and the microcosm are intimately related. There is nothing in the policy of my nation that I do not recognise in myself. How do I weigh a costly home insurance policy against the needs of a young struggling mother with three children who has no home at all, not in Capetown, but within half a mile of my house? Or running a car? Or even buying a cinema ticket?

Personal responsibility and public decision-making are not of a different order. How does one weigh the equipment of hospitals for expensive surgery against the use of finite resources for preventive medicine? It can be argued that the personal answers are easier than the political ones? Do our lives bear that out?

I believe that those who say that my childhood trauma can finally only be answered by converting everybody to Jesus are wrong. Personal sanctity – however widespread – cannot heal all the wounds of broken humanity. Even more to the point, it simply has to be admitted that individually and collectively the converted have no better record than humanity in general. If only it could be said that Christianity and moral sensitivity to the needs of humanity go hand in hand. To place the peace of the world in the hands of people on the grounds that they can with honesty claim to be Christian would be wildly irresponsible. Christians are in no way immune from blindness, fear, prejudice or any of the other vices that make people so dangerous to each other. Nor are they any better at resisting the corrupting temptations of power.

If that is true so is the converse. Karl Marx who was right about so many things – more right than nearly all the Christians of his time – was nevertheless wrong in assuming that all our ills, all human alienation (a better word than sin), springs from social and economic injustice. Only get social structures right and all will be well, and true harmony, true peace will be established. The dream is as false as the evangelical preacher's trust in individual conversion. Utopian politics are a recipe for disaster.

What hope at all then? There is no ground for any kind of easy optimism. But hope is different. Hope in every human situation points to the possibility of the apparently impossible. Nuclear war is more probable than nuclear disarmament. But neither are impossible. For a long time there may be neither, time within which a fragment of the cosmic struggle between good and evil is fought out. And there will be no easy agreement who is on which side. What Jesus called the Kingdom is already in evidence every time, in matters small and great, that love gets the better of fear and forgiveness gets the better of hatred. Those who actually make the Kingdom come will often be those from whom it is least expected (those damned Samaritans again!) and who would not recognise themselves in that role. The kindly cynics are often capable of a good deal more practical love than the dedicated idealists.

And as for the almost universal tendency to blame the world's troubles on its rulers, it cuts no ice with me. To be critical of the misuse of power is necessary, often harshly critical, but such criticism is essentially no different from the self-criticism that goes with being a reasonably mature human being. I return at this point to the concept of critical solidarity which should characterise all our relationships, including those with ourselves.

Writing as I am in London, in 1986, my dismay and often anger at the policies of Margaret Thatcher's government are much greater than at those of any of its predecessors. I shall go on fighting them. But I recognise in those policies and the people implementing them characteristics that are widespread throughout Britain. I have often said that if power was transferred from Downing Street to Coronation Street – or to my own street – I am not at all sure that our ills would be decreased or peace made more secure. A little self-knowledge, and the stories of Adam and Eve and Cain and Abel, should surely suffice to rid us of romantic notions about 'the common man' – if I may risk such sexist language. The much more serious and proper point, that power has for far too long in human history been concentrated in male hands is certainly not the answer either, but a very important part of it, and one (not the only one) to which the Churches remain much more resistant than the world.

The alternatives politicians face are real, but always limited. Yet not quite as limited as it seems to them. People and pressure-groups are necessary to help them expand the vision of what is possible. Yet the extremest options are not always the most radical, do not always get to the root of the problem. To help politicians to do that will not make for popularity, but that is what Christian prophecy is about: pointing out reality, however unpalatable it may be. Nor will the middle ground necessarily provide the answers. Jesus, and this bears repetition, would never have been described as a 'moderate'.

Is there a Christian answer to the contemporary choice for Britain between a socialist and a market economy? The absolute free market and the totally socialised society are – in practice – alternative forms of tyranny. As developmental stages on the way to something more humane and more just both are defensible, in theory. But the risks to humanity are too great, in both cases.

A society based on common ownership yet incorporating

large areas of free enterprise and of cultural freedom is one ideal, the one that almost certainly comes closest to the spirit of the Sermon on the Mount and the Acts of the Apostles. It is the kind of society that, conceivably, Alexander Dubcek's 'socialism with a human face' might have achieved in Czechoslovakia, had it not been crushed by Soviet tanks. It is the kind of society that might have been achievable in Salvador Allende's Chile or even in today's Nicaragua were it not for the power of American capitalism.

The same end is as thinkable in a market economy that is strictly geared to social priorities, that accepts a substantial redistribution of wealth, arbitration between competing interest groups and the prevention of powerful monopolies.

It may be that what I have attempted, in very brief compass, to describe is the option between democratic socialism and social democracy. Both, politics with a human face. The future may produce better models. These, for the present, in many variations, could be made to work for the benefit of all people everywhere, ensuring a minimum of social, economic and political rights. The world is far from that goal. We are still, nationally and even more internationally, traumatically trapped 'under the ship's engines'.

5

In Hitler's Mercedes

Returning to my birthplace was a problem. I had left it, with Hitler in power, in order to survive. Sixteen years later it was no longer part of the 'western world' and the cold war was at its height. It lay just inside the border of the German Democratic Republic, but no one in Bonn, where I was a research student, called it that. It was part of the Soviet Zone. To West Germans simply *drüben*, 'over there'. Over there my surviving grandmother was not far from death in an old people's home. I applied to the GDR authorities in Berlin for a visitor's visa. Three months later the answer was 'no'.

Angry and frustrated, I bought a visa, as anyone could, to the Leipzig Trade Fair. Once in Leipzig I went to the police headquarters and there asked permission to visit my grandmother on the way back to the West. A two-hour wait was followed by instructions to report to a room on the fifth floor to discuss the matter further. The door was labelled 'Consul of the USSR'. This must be a mistake, I thought. My grandmother lives here in East Germany, not in Russia. I went downstairs again to point this out. This time I was not politely asked to go to the fifth floor but told: 'If you don't go, we'll take you.'

I knocked. The Soviet official was waiting for me. He was a lot more than a consul. This was the beginning of an arduous, two-day cross examination by the KGB. I was in fact being detained as a suspected spy, though the polite fiction was maintained throughout, that my interrogator was 'helping me in my wish to see my grandmother'. In fact she was assumed to be a pretext to visit the border area. And I was apparently assumed to be a West German with a false New Zealand passport. That day and the next were probably my longest ever. I feared for my life. If my story did not cohere in every detail, I might well disappear into what the world now calls the Gulag. My one and only slight advantage over 'the consul' was that I spoke German better than he did. It gave me a little more thinking time. And I learnt how, in such a thorough interrogation, one lapse would quickly have pitted me into a web of contradictions. I could even, at moments, begin to appreciate my adversary's craft. He was doing his job with skill.

As day two was drawing to a close the tone just slightly changed. 'I think you can visit your grandmother.' Was I really in the clear? 'When!', I asked. 'Not now. You should not be in Leipzig at all. We will put you on the next train back to the West. Then you can apply again to see your grandmother.' The relief was tremendous. He believed me! 'But why then,' I asked, 'will you not let me visit my grandmother now?' For a moment he dropped his official mask and looked at me sadly, almost appealingly, and said: 'You must understand. I can see no reason why you should not visit your grandmother. But what if you are cleverer than me? What if I am wrong, and let you go there? What will happen to me?' His simple gesture then signified that he would not survive. When we shook hands, for the first and last time, we had reason to be sorry for each other. Now it had become easy to embrace him in my prayers. Before that it had been very hard. Two human beings parting.

Looking back, I would not have missed that experience for anything. Never again would I make easy, negative judgements about those in all our systems of state security, who hold the lives of others in their hands. That many are cruel and corrupt cannot be denied. But it must never simply be assumed. My interrogator, whose name I was never told, was as frightened as I was and in many ways more of a prisoner than I. In much of the moving literature stemming from the experiences of prisoners of conscience there is evidence that the prisoner often feels more free than his gaolers. I had begun to understand what that means. In my prayers for the tortured and persecuted I have gradually come to recognise that those who are the cause of their suffering need the prayers and the compassion of the Church most of all. And having prayed, I know only too well that 'there but for the grace of God, go I'.

That story had two very different sequels. There was no reason known to me why my path and the KGB's should ever cross again. They did, nearly thirty years later, though, at the time, I did not know it. Nor was I now in any danger. The diplomat at the Soviet Embassy in London responsible for liaison with Churches and peace organisations was Oleg Gordievsky. As the British Council of Churches' international secretary and as a Vice-President of the Campaign for Nuclear Disarmament it was natural that I should meet him, as I also met his American counterpart. In a strange way he reminded me of my Leipzig 'diplomat'. I enjoyed his company and our conversations went well beyond his official brief. He was interested in the life of the Spirit. He brought his wife to our home. What could I give him in exchange for good Russian vodka? He wanted a Russian Bible concordance.

Then suddenly, we could meet no more and probably never again. The press revealed that he was a double agent, working for Soviet and British security. Had I been duped? Not really. Any diplomat, I knew well enough, might not *only* be a diplomat. Only the double role seemed closer to fiction than to reality. That relationship, which bordered on friendship, made me realise again how readily society traps us into making superficial judgements. Spies are needed and employed by every nation, and yet treated – when exposed – like criminals, or like prostitutes who are assumed to be indispensable and yet despised. Agents and double agents no doubt have mixed motives – as we all have – but the more I reflect on their role, the more I come to believe that the world is marginally safer when governments know what their potential opponents do not want them to know. Nothing breeds greater fear than the ignorance which forces us to make the worst possible assumptions about our opponents. While a host of official secrets characterise most governments – though some a lot more than others – breaking them down is not to be entirely despised.

But lest I be misunderstood: nothing would please me more than the demise of the KGB and all its national equivalents. That would be the beginning of a more human world. Meanwhile, I pray that if there have to be spies and interrogators, let them be good and intelligent ones. The other kind are a real menace.

And now the happier sequel to my detention. The one that led, eventually, to my grandmother. Not long after my return to West Germany the German Protestant Church's Lay Congress – the Kirchentag of 1956 – took place in Frankfurt. It was one of the last to which a whole train-load of Christians was allowed by their authorities to come from the East. Leading them were two Christian politicians from the GDR: Johannes Diekmann, Speaker of the East German Parliament, and Otto Nuschke, Deputy Prime Minister and leader of the Christian Democratic Union in the GDR. Neither were communists, both belonged to the small parties still allowed in the GDR which represent what are regarded as minority interests. Their influence was and remains small.

In a mass meeting of some three thousand people the Kirchentag, one afternoon, discussed the future of Germany. A panel of speakers were to give differing views. Otto Nuschke was one of them. He was elderly. Not a great man, but one with an impeccable democratic record of opposition to Hitler. At the height of the cold war it seemed significant that he should be free to explain in West Germany why he felt it right, as a Christian, to hold office in the East German government. Not many shared his position. He would not expect to find many sympathisers among Christians in East or West Germany. But it was a lot worse for him than that. The bitterness and intensity of West German anti-communism, not least among Christians, was much greater than the organisers had bargained with. Today, thirty years later, the scene that ensued would be quite unthinkable. The crowd simply shouted Otto Nuschke down with cries of traitor. The chairman's plea for dialogue and tolerance was received with angry disdain. I sat at the back, shocked and frightened by an atmosphere all too reminiscent of the days of Hitler's rule.

Sadly, yet with his dignity intact, the old man who now seemed older than his years left the hall. Deeply disturbed, somehow ashamed to be identified with this audience, I and a handful of others followed Dr Nuschke out. He got into his car. In a taxi, I followed him to his hotel. There I asked, would he be prepared to see me? In his room I explained who I was and how ashamed that he should be so treated in what prided in calling itself the 'free world'. 'I have lived long enough not to be surprised by anything,' he said, smiling. 'Then let me tell you,' I continued, 'what happened to me in your State a few weeks ago.' He was not surprised at the story of my grandmother and the KGB either. 'In this climate of cold war and fear,' he said, 'terrible things happen. Much worse things than your experience. I have little power to change all that but enough to get you to your grandmother whenever you choose.' He need not have trusted me, but he did. And kept his word.

Two weeks later I handed his secretary my passport in East Berlin and had a visa within two hours. Not only that: his chauffeur was waiting downstairs to drive me to the other end of the country, a four- to five-hour journey on the autobahn that Hitler had built. I wondered, was the driver being sent with me to keep an eye on me? My question was anticipated. 'When you get to your birthplace, to Meiningen, do as you wish. Ask the driver to wait for you or send him back alone and return by train when you like.'

The car that was waiting for me downstairs was the ultimate irony. An elderly chauffeur in a leather greatcoat held the door for me as though I were some high guest of state. And the car? One of the fleet of special design Mercedes-Benz limousines which Hitler had ordered for the top Nazi leaders. I didn't know whether to laugh or cry. This and others like it must have been inherited by the East German leadership. Today these cars could be sold for vast sums, and maybe have been, to western film studios. The driver had started as a government chauffeur during the Weimar Republic, had driven the Nazis

and now Otto Nuschke. A refreshing Berlin 'cockney', he
regaled me with stories all the way, delighted, as he put it, to
be driving an ordinary human being for a change.

And so to my grandmother. She was to live only a few
months longer. My second visit to East Germany in embarrassing 'state' was as bizarre as my frightening first. I have been
back to the GDR every year since. Over those thirty years the
country, and its people among whom I was born, have again
become an integral part of my life.

Through no other sustained aspect of my ministry could I
better demonstrate to myself and to others my understanding
of reconciliation and peace. What made me return again and
again, building up a network of relationships paralleled
nowhere else in my ministry? To begin with, it was all deeply
personal: the need to come to terms spiritually with the people
who had robbed my parents of their home; people whose children my paediatrician father had healed but who would no
longer recognise him on the street, because his parents were
Jews; people who were responsible for the suicide of my
father's mother on the eve of her intended deportation to the
death camps in Poland. Some I had cause to resent personally.
Most I did not know by name. But between me and those few
who had had the courage to stand by our family there was a
deep bond. The need to relate positively to all these people,
both gratitude to some and the wish to forgive others, was the
beginning of a long-lasting GDR pilgrimage. Nearer the
surface, there was the knowledge that here was a country in
the Soviet camp with which I had at least some personal affinity
and in which my conviction that Christians and Communists
must be in dialogue, must learn to respect and perhaps even
love each other, could be practically tested.

Here was another context, a place rejected and despised by
most of the outside world, where I could test my own convic-
tions about critical solidarity with others. I could no more
embrace the GDR than reject it. Yet could I somehow help to
build bridges between its Christians and its Communists and
people in Britain, where I had made my home? It proved

possible and rewarding. Personal resentments were overcome. They had to be, for the sake of things that really mattered.

Yet how does one move freely across a society that is so polarised? Could I befriend Christians and also befriend those who, in none too humane ways, held sway over them? Could I accept an invitation from those in power and then, on my next visit, befriend their sternest critics? Could I, as the Chairman of the British Section of Amnesty International, work for the release of those wrongfully imprisoned in the GDR and then bring a delegation of senior British Christians to visit the churches of the GDR? Could I develop relationships of trust with people so far apart that they would never trust each other?

All this has proved possible and continues to be. But it is also beset by many hazards. For every success, from the setting free of a prominent political prisoner in the early sixties to the completion of a television film on the life of the Church in the early eighties, there have been setbacks and disappointments. For every shared achievement, there has been shared failure. For all the realisation that life can be lived positively and creatively in this Marxist-Leninist society, there has also been the painful reality that for some of my closest friends that life had become intolerable. Some have emigrated with my help.

I have, over the years, had the privilege of getting to know well most of the GDR's Protestant Church leaders. Some have become close friends. I have been made to feel almost an honorary member of a remarkably lively and challenging Roman Catholic parish. I count among my friends leading members of the Christian Democratic Union, the successors to Otto Nuschke who made my first visit possible. And I have been able to establish a relationship of friendship and trust with a number of leading Communists, most particularly the last and the present Secretaries of State for Church Affairs.

But I have also had to learn that, even taken together, all these people do not express the mood of most ordinary people who are neither Christians nor Communists. It was a local Communist party secretary who said to the Dean of the Lutheran Cathedral: 'Pastor, you can count on about 3% of the people; we can count on about the same number. And we are both equally worried about the other 94%.' That was unusually honest. For me it has not been as easy to meet a cross-section of these 94%, but it has not been impossible. Family holidays have made it a little easier and so has taking time simply to drive around the country. Meeting a cross-section of young people where they congregate, usually listening to music, has often been an eye-opener and has led to instructive friendships.

And then there have been those on the very edge of society. 'Dissidents' would only describe some of them. Others simply want to be left alone by State and Church to be themselves. Others, again, are on fire for peace (as they and not the State understands it) or for the preservation of the environment. Nearly all have one thing in common: the deep wish to be part of a wider world, not bounded by the closed frontiers of the GDR. Again and again I came to see how – despite superficial differences – all these people have so much in common with their counterparts in Britain. At those moments my British debates with men like Lord Chalfont loom large in my mind. It was he who said at a public meeting: 'I would rather shoot my children dead than let them grow up in a Communist ruled country.' That is exactly what Hitler's propaganda minister, Josef Goebbels, did when the Russians marched into Berlin. It reflects ultimate fear, bereft of faith, hope and love.

Even those in the West who are less melodramatic live with an image of a vast grey brainwashed world stretching from Berlin to Vladivostok simply called 'behind the iron curtain'. That takes no account of the riches of human nature. If we really imagine that the daily lives of ordinary Russians and Poles and Czechs are so different from our own, we vastly overestimate the power of systems to crush the human spirit. If laughter and tears could be measured (as suicide statistics can) we would find hardly any difference between Eastern and Western Europe.

Of course that doesn't mean that one political system is as good as another. Given freedom to choose, the majority of the people of Eastern Europe would choose a system more like our own, just as the majority of people in Latin America would choose a socialist one.

History does not stand still. Democracies and tyrannies do not last for ever. Life itself is a form of change, sometimes rapid, sometimes hardly perceived. But beneath that there are enduring values. The life of the Spirit – again, that Bird of Heaven – cannot be contained by systems. The young poet I found living in a GDR church-tower, above the belfry, will go on writing poetry. It may or may not be published, but no one will stop him.

And everywhere there are the two or three (sometimes two or three thousand) gathered in Christ's name to break bread, to celebrate resurrection, life that is new each day, life to be enjoyed and life to be suffered. And always people to be loved.

There is not one way of doing that, but many. Openness to the Spirit, wherever we happen to be, is to listen to the inner voice, to be still and to let the Inner Light of Christ shine, and then to make our choices, to discover our way of living. And even when life leaves us with no choices, there is still the question of how we tread the path chosen for us.

My Christian friends in the GDR do not all make the same choices. Some choose to live very private lives. Some, sensitive to the injustices of their system, have the courage to oppose it and to suffer the consequences. Some, more aware of the historic sins of Christendom against the working classes, are convinced that it is only through working in and through their system, however imperfect, that they can commend Christ and help build a more humane kind of socialism. These are not right and wrong options. The sadness is that – wherever it may be – we so often refuse to honour and even learn from the choices of others. German culture and tradition make that even more difficult than it is for most people in Britain. 'If my decision is right, then surely a different one must be wrong!' When others have shared their spiritual gifts and insights with me, I have often, in return, been able to suggest that my way (and my own nature has always been to choose one with clarity) is not necessarily the best for others, even for those close to me. The older I get the more it seems to me that the truth, or at any rate fragments of the truth, is generally to be found in opposites.

Nowhere do I feel more at ease and at home than among those, be it in East or West, who pit their lives against the militarist monster that threatens to engulf our planet. When that monster claims to be the true peace movement, perversity seems to have climaxed. That is a heavy cross for young East German Christians, who refuse to bow down to a state god called Peace. Nothing unifies many young Germans in East and West more surely than their determination not to be conscripted into the armies of NATO and the Warsaw Pact, with their vast nuclear arsenals. That form of resistance is far more costly on the Communist-ruled side, but – to its credit – the East German State does make some allowance for it, alone among its allies.

However, much of the moral fervour of young – and not so young – anti-militarists, much of their natural passion, goes into hating the people and structures who represent power in their own society. That produces the paradox that professional soldiers, specially those who have seen war, are often more peaceable personalities than the committed 'fighters for peace'. If there is any justification for specifically Christian peace groups in a wider movement, it is to help save those trying to combat the creation of enemy images from doing just that themselves. In Britain in 1986, to begin an address to a mainly youthful CND rally (as I have done) with the words, 'We are not in this against Margaret Thatcher and Ronald Reagan but for all people, everywhere', is to risk not being listened to.

This was borne in on me even more powerfully at a 'peace workshop' under Church auspices in a suburb of East Berlin. Some two or three thousand young people had gathered to express their feelings about the system in which they lived. These were angry young people, as angry about Soviet military power as young CND activists are about American Cruise missiles in Britain.

In one corner of a huge church garden a large notice, in English, announced that this was *Speakers' Corner*. Here was an oasis of totally free speech. Little that they felt was left unsaid. Suddenly one of the young people said to me: 'Don't you have a message for us from the West?' My Taizé cross, in the shape of a dove, was already, I had hoped, some kind of non-verbal signal. 'All right,' I said, 'but you may not like my message: I welcome your resistance to the militarism of your society and hope that, if I lived here, I would have your kind of courage. But you can do more for peace than that. Almost every town in the GDR has its Soviet garrison. The officers and their families live among you. Yet they are totally isolated from you, their German neighbours. Human contact is confined to officially sponsored "friendship meetings". Why don't you start breaking that barrier down? You were all forced to learn some Russian at school. Why not get over your anti-Soviet complexes and *use* a little of that Russian? Why not, when you next see a Russian family on the street, wish them a good day in their own language?'

There was a long silence. Was it one of perplexity or of resentment? Was I being fair, I wondered? How many British peace campaigners have invited American service families to their homes? But, on reflection, I knew I'd said the right thing. This was my critical solidarity with a group of very fine young people. The gospel is there to disturb the best of them – and us.

After the long silence, a well-known dissident Communist writer, who had been listening, had the wit to suggest: 'Well then, we'd better found our own GDR-Soviet Friendship Society' – many of those present had no doubt already been enrolled in the official one. The crowd fell about laughing.

Will the Chalfonts of this world ever learn that things are never quite what they seem to be? They will have to travel a long way to find the brainwashed world of their fantasies.

6

In Prison with Terrorists

'We believe, Canon, you visit terrorists in prison in your spare time?' The setting was the Grocers' Hall in the City of London. I was being interviewed by the largely absentee churchwardens of St Mary-le-Bow to discover whether I might make a suitable rector. Actually they had long ago made up their mind that the Archbishop of Canterbury must have put my name forward in a momentary fit of summer madness. I was able to reassure them, as a liveried butler served tea, that if I did take the job, I would not give the City half as much to worry about as Jesus had given the City of Jerusalem. What made me feel ashamed is that I was not really the radical they were assuming. Would that I deserved my reputation. Despite my gratitude to the Archbishop, I said no to the job. I hope it wasn't only out of cowardice.

But they were right to ask me about visiting terrorists. I had not long before spent a lot of time – though not spare time – with terrorists. The situation in West Germany had reached a stage of virtual desperation. Some forty imprisoned members or alleged members – many still awaiting trial – of the Baader-Meinhof Gang, or as they called themselves the Red Army Faction, had gone on hunger strike. One of them, Holger Meins, had died. As a reprisal, a Berlin court judge had been murdered. Many more deaths were feared.

The families of the prisoners approached me through the sister of one of them. Would I offer my services as a mediator between the State and the prisoners, with only one objective, that the hunger strike, which had brought many of them close to death, should end? It was not an easy decision. These were not in any acceptable sense prisoners of conscience. Would I, as Chairman of Amnesty International's British Section, by helping in this way, give the impression that they were, in fact, Amnesty cases?

In the end the possibility of saving lives took precedence over everything else. I said yes, provided I was simply going as a priest and my mission was given no publicity. And provided, of course, that the West German government and the prisoners were prepared to accept me in that role.

In the two weeks that followed I found myself commuting between prison cells in Stuttgart, Hamburg and Berlin and the office of the Federal State Prosecutor in Karlsruhe. It was, for me, the hardest ever test of openness to human beings, for I could identify with none of them. But could I think and, even more importantly, feel myself into their position? Success – or even partial success – would depend on that. It had to be possible. But how, I had no idea. Faced with that kind of mission, the temptation to pray the wrong kind of prayer was great, the kind of prayer that passes the buck back to God. That is always an evasion of our own responsibility and a fear of the consequences of our own failure.

The spiritual dimension of this mission was not in principle different from that in all other human encounters. The practical difference – and it was enormous – was that I was suddenly catapulted into a world of top-level state security on the one hand and surrealistic revolutionary utopianism on the other. That called for a radical readjustment to realms in which the abnormal becomes normal. Where could God be in all this? Not somewhere 'out there' with power to intervene, not a divine puppeteer with invisible strings going into cells and law courts and high offices of state, but a God living and suffering, and perhaps dying, within every person involved in this tragedy.

In Hamburg's remand prison I was not taken to the cells. The prisoners were brought to meet me across a long table in an interview room. Framed on the wall facing me, behind the prisoners, were words by Dietrich Bonhoeffer which I did not forget during those exhausting weeks: 'You will never enhance the humanity of someone you despise.' Perhaps not strangely, by the end, the only people I was tempted to despise were some of the defendants' manipulative lawyers and the unscrupulous journalists to whom the hunger strike and my mission, which they came close to wrecking, was just one more lucrative story.

And I learnt, during those weeks, the force of something Victor Hugo had once written: 'Not the quality of its churches but of its prisons defines the quality of a nation's life.' At one level, the hunger strike *was* about the quality of West German prisons. The members of the Red Army Faction were in open revolt at their treatment as terrorists and were demanding, among other things, to be brought together and held as political prisoners. At another level, the prisoners were simply continuing their battle against society in any way they could.

As in any such conflict, was there any chance of getting the two sides to make minimal concessions to each other? Neither could afford to lose face. The prisoners had their morale and solidarity to maintain; the authorities could not, in the light of public opinion, even appear to be making concessions. But there were areas of possible compromise open to both sides. They threatened neither the prisoners' morale on the one hand nor state security on the other. And so, in the end – with my role as only one factor – the hunger strike did end without further loss of life.

What had I learnt? This, above all, that even terrorists and professional anti-terrorists remain individual persons, very different from each other. Collective judgements about a terrorist movement are possible, or about a prison system, but to lump all the people together fails, as we so often do, to take the uniqueness of the human personality into account.

The best and the worst in human nature are not far separated. Idealism and fanatacism are very closely related. The mainly young, emaciated men and women I was visiting, usually in their cells, were both idealists and fanatics with the kind of self-righteousness that is not too rare in people of passionate religious conviction either. One of the few things nearly all the prisoners had in common was a certainty that they were the moral superiors, not only of their captors, but of the whole of society. The fact that very few people shared their burning zeal to destroy, before a new society could be born, made them all the more sure they must be right. The paths that led them to this point could not have been more diverse. They ranged from philosophers of some depth to dare-devil adventurers, yet virtually all equally deluded that they were the forerunners of tomorrow's revolution. One day, they were persuaded, the world would honour them.

Religion, I had much cause to reflect, is also an expression of both the best and the worst in individuals and in society; religion, that is, in its purer strains, abstracted from the correctives created by the ordinariness of life. There is only a thin line between sanctity and insanity, between holiness and obsession. Loyalty to a vision can so easily be a cover for letting loose our aggressions and working off our fears on all who fail to share that vision.

Among the committed followers of Ulrike Meinhof and Andreas Baader were several whose youthful idealism had been deeply religious. None more so than the strongest woman in the group, Andreas Baader's mentor and lover, Gudrun Ensslin. She was able to justify her principled stand, her violent rejection of the status quo and her willingness to die for a better future, in language that was reminiscent of the fundamentalist puritanism of the Festival of Light. The God of her evangelical upbringing had disappointed her, had not delivered, but the emotional and intellectual framework in which she had encountered that God was left intact. Her morale was high, even when she was close to death, high enough to inspire others, in other prison cells.

No meeting during those weeks made me reflect more deeply than that with Gudrun Ensslin's parents; her father, a devoted Lutheran pastor, his wife the almost archetypal 'good Christian woman'. Frau Ensslin understood only too well the full extent of the tragedy of her daughter. 'If only,' she said to me weeping, 'we had not brought Gudrun up so piously.' Does that, then, argue against Christian commitment? Against a religion that is more than lukewarm? Against a vision of God that demands the response of the whole personality?

I sympathise with those who think that it does. My heart goes out to the many whose lives have been wounded by religion in many of its destructive forms, by religion that is either an escape from reality or an unbending attempt to make reality conform to some moral or dogmatic principle. I am not shocked beyond measure when, as would-be socialist heirs to the Enlightenment, the rulers of the Soviet Union legislate about religion as we (and they) legislate about pornography. Its consumption is permitted to consenting adults on licensed premises or in private. It is held to be harmful to children. Consumed by whole societies, it is thought to lead to war. And the assumption is that it has, in a major way, contributed to the subjugation of women, to sexual neurosis and to personal bitterness.

It is fashionable in Christian circles to shrug off such criticism as Marxist or Freudian old hat, because Marx and Freud are gods that have also failed. But it is not necessary to summon these two prophets-of-their-time to damn religion. Jesus will do. He did it with much greater penetration and was executed for it.

What is the difference between the total dedication of a Gudrun Ensslin and the equal dedication of a Daniel Berrigan? Dedication even to comparable objectives? The short answer is that the one had a sense of humour and the other did not. The saint knows himself to be a fallible sinner and will never mistake himself for God. He will never take himself so seriously that there is no room for self-deprecating laughter. The saint, having realistic expectations of him or herself, is also less liable than the zealot to lapse into depression. The saint does not depend on success, any more than Jesus did.

That does raise the question why the Jesus of the New Testament is permitted to weep but not to laugh. I suspect that it tells us more about St Paul and the evangelists than it tells us about Jesus. The effect on most Christian theologians has been disastrous and, in turn, on the Church. So determined were the New Testament writers to stress the 'otherness' of Jesus that the wisdom of rabbinical humour was quite lost. The maturing process of the twentieth century's greatest theologian, Karl Barth, illustrates well what I mean. Barth began as the stern, dogmatic affirmer of revealed truth, he ended as the warm self-deprecating ('I am no Barthian!') affirmer of the humanity of God who felt closest to reality when listening to Mozart or sharing his vision of divine love with the prisoners of Basel's jail in simple, down-to-earth sermons. The young and the old Barth were two different people, as were the young and old Marx, who regrettably moved in the opposite direction. A passionate and compassionate young journalist became a near infallible law-giver. With the sad result that many aspects of Marxism soon came to resemble the worst aspects of the religion it had discarded.

The priest at the sick-bed, even at the death bed, knows well how those who are close to God are often, even when in pain, capable of laughter. Such laughter, not least the ribaldry of hospital laughter, found no place in my visits to the prisoners from the German terrorist scene. Some of them were close to death. To prove the rightness of their cause to me was all that really mattered, and to show their disdain for my assumed subservience to bourgeois values.

My assumed questioning of these values was, it must be said, treated with equal disdain, though with much greater politeness, by the representatives of the State which enshrines these values. Not much humour there, either. Even so, the protagonists on both sides *were* sufficiently human to take me seriously as a person, even when they suspected that I was dangerously close to 'the enemy'. Paradoxically, they were both right in making such an assumption.

If the cross I shared with the fanatical prisoners, the harassed prison staff and the terrified state authorities was closely related to the failure of 'Christian' society to reflect the good news of human liberation, there was a different kind of sharing with the one prisoner with whom I could truly empathise. Ulrike Meinhof was quite unlike the others. She was no longer even in solidarity with them. To be with her was to be in the hell of total despair. I could relate her despair to Jesus' cry of dereliction on the cross. She was beyond crying. We communicated almost entirely in silence. I partly understood because I knew something of the story of her pilgrimage to hell.

She too had been brought up as a devout Christian by a strict and dedicated pacifist step-mother who was also a formidable intellectual with high expectations of her adopted daughter. And they were fulfilled. Ulrike became one of West Germany's most respected liberal television journalists. Her documentaries on social concerns were formative for a whole generation of young, idealistic radicals. And she was beautiful. Married to a wealthy publisher. The mother of twins. She had the makings of a German Jane Fonda. But her idealism began to eat away at her soul. She was disgusted at her good life. At the profit she was taking from the misery of those who had no hope of sharing that life. Would her documentaries change anything while she remained the darling of the chic, pseudo-radical Hamburg high society epitomised by her wealthy husband?

One night she abandoned it all. Children, marriage, world and status. Through her eyes, doing a St Francis. She went to live in a pacifist commune. But soon the dream of self-sacrificing non-violence went sour too. Was it not just an alternative form of self-indulgence? In her new life-style she was doing even less to liberate the world's poor. Flower-power and self-denial were not the road to the Kingdom either. She moved into the revolutionary scene of the late sixties. Her hero now was Ché Guevara. Liberation would have to come out of the barrel of a gun. And not just in the Third World. Andreas Baader, a young romantic dreamer with not an intellectual notion in his head, now found a partner in Ulrike who had both glamour and dedication and could help him to understand Lenin and Mao and Marcuse and, in Gudrun Ensslin, a lover with an even sharper intellect. Little more was needed to attract others and to begin to change the world. And so the campaign of murder directed at the capitalist system began. And led . . . nowhere. Ulrike Meinhof was the only one of the prisoners to acknowledge to herself that each step of renunciation had been a failure. Nothing had been of any use. Not even her hunger strike. The others knew that she had spiritually surrendered. She did not care whether she lived or died. She was beyond that. And I knew – or thought I knew – that any talk of God would have been a final act of cruelty. For it was to satisfy the demands of this very god that she had set out on her journey to hell. I could do no more than share her emptiness of soul, not knowing whether before me was a lost sinner or a redeemed soul sharing hell with Jesus. The mystery was too deep. Of only one thing was I as sure as any person can ever be: whatever might happen to the others, she would die.

When the others began to eat again, so did she. But she remained an outcast. Not very much later she hanged herself. If there is no place for her in paradise, on the long road back to the Father, I doubt if there is one for me.

When a journalist on the news magazine *Spiegel* publicised my mission, he effectively also put an end to it. The prisoners were, by now, in any case determined to go on living in order to fight another round. I had done what I could. They were no longer willing to talk to me. They were not going to hand any credit for ending the hunger strike to some British middle-class parson who wasn't committed to their cause. Why should they?

Now my role would be – for a day or two – a different one. A public one. It was almost Christmas. On *Panorama* and other, German, TV and radio programmes I countered, as best I could, the fanatical hatred a large section of the West German public felt for the prisoners. Many people had hoped they would starve themselves to death. I had no choice but to share my conviction that in these prisoners too the image of God remained alive, however much obscured. Not one of them was beyond redemption. To wish them dead was a fascist, not a Christian response. I had praise, too, for many officials of the prison service who, hard as they must have found it, acted on that kind of assumption, though few of them would have used my kind of language to express it. Few of them deserved the abuse heaped indiscriminately on them all by the ideological left.

For my refusal to dehumanise either side, I expected little public sympathy. It was all the more heart-warming for me when, doing some Christmas shopping in a Hamburg department store before flying back to London, total strangers came up to me, took my hand and simply said 'thank you'. At least some knew what Christmas was really about. And Good Friday. And Easter. I could not ask for more.

Neither could I lose sight of reality. Be it in Germany or in Britain or anywhere else in the Western world, those who are more concerned with the underlying causes of violent protest than with eliminating the perpetrators are a small minority. When churchwardens in the City of London asked me was it true that I visit terrorists in prison, the clear implication was that this was not the kind of thing a respectable clergyman should be up to. Indeed, when the brave and prophetic Lutheran Bishop of Berlin visited Ulrike Meinhof in prison as a basic pastoral duty, the right-wing tabloid *Bildzeitung* appeared the next day with the libellous headline: 'Scharf, Bishop of Terror'.

There remains a profound reluctance on the part of most Christians individually and of our Churches as institutions to identify with those whom society rejects, regardless of what their alleged sin might be. Jesus was constantly putting his good name at risk for keeping bad company.

It is in this context – the context of where we all stand as ordinary men and women – that my experience has universal relevance. Very few of us in the world of our work and of our private life are not at sometime or other faced with the question of sacrificing our reputation, for standing by someone who would otherwise remain alone. That person may not deserve our friendship. All the more reason to offer it.

In the sacrament of Holy Communion God in Christ offers every sinner who chooses to accept the offer, not just friendship, but his own life. The offer is as open to a convicted murderer in one of Her Majesty's prisons as it is to the Queen.

The Queen is not brought down to the level of the prisoner. Both together are raised to the level of God. We are still very far from showing that we understand what that means. In a nation as addicted to ceremonies and as devoted to royalty as Britain, it would speak loud and clear if the nation's Sovereign and the Church's titular lay head, its 'Supreme Governor', were, as part of her ministry, to worship from time to time in one of her prisons and to kneel, as a forgiven sinner, beside another forgiven sinner, who may well be a convicted terrorist. Here would be a symbolic demonstration of the meaning of God's free grace. Free, but not cheap.

Just how hard it is for ordinary people to accept the implications of our common humanity came home to me with depressing clarity on my visit to two of the terrorist prisoners who were so weak, so close to death, that they had been flown in a helicopter to the university hospital in Mainz. So precarious was the security situation that a whole hospital-block was cleared to house these two men, hovering between life and death. It was surrounded by barbed wire and troops.

That particular hospital was chosen because of the almost unique skills of the Professor of Anaesthetics in near terminal life-management. He undertook to care for the two men provided his medical integrity was totally respected. 'They will be my patients like all others. I shall take orders about them from no one, and I shall not force any treatment on them. I shall try to keep them alive, but only with their consent.'

The question then was, who would work with the professor? No member of the hospital staff, he insisted, should be compelled to. An appeal was made to the whole medical and nursing staff, many hundreds of people. Only seven volunteered. Only just enough to maintain round-the-clock intensive care. One was the hospital's medical director, another a junior doctor and five were nursing staff. Given the ethics of the medical profession, the high calling to heal all people, regardless of who they are, one would hope that all would have been ready to volunteer. In fact those seven and above all the professor with his profound reverence for life, by volunteering to save the lives of these terrorists, but also by refusing to force-feed them, had saved the hospital's and the German medical profession's honour.

How many hundreds of practising Christians were there, I wonder, on the staff of that hospital? Seven, who may or may not have been Christians, carried the cross for them all. The prisoners lived.

There is no happy end to this story. No discernible redemption of this personal, social and political tragedy. Ulrike Meinhof's suicide was followed by the violent deaths of Andreas Baader, of Gudrun Ensslin and of Jan-Karl Raspe. The official version is that they shot themselves. The unofficial version is that they were murdered. Both scenarios seem improbable. One of them must be true. Only a very few people will know for sure which it was. Ingrid Schubert was one more of those I had visited. A young idealistic doctor, she later took her own life. It was to her sister that I owed the costly privilege of sharing in this human drama. And not only were the leaders of the Red Army Faction dead. Dr Buback, the Chief State Prosecutor with whom I had long conferred, died too, murdered.

In the houses and streets and prisons of Ulster an even greater tragedy goes on being played out day by day, week by week. There are many heroic, open Christians, men and women like the Mainz anaesthetist, in the midst of that conflict. But there are many others who constitute the real problem. What is that problem?

Not terrorism as such. Nor the people described as terrorists. There is nothing new about the concept or about the people. It has gone by many names. The problem, I believe, is – at its core – the refusal of human society, including most of its Christian components, to take the concept of reverence for life seriously.

If the interests of one's nation, or class or race or religion is a more sacred cause than the preservation of life, then the pass that leads to terrorism has been sold. If 'the defence of the realm' justifies war, in which innocent and guilty invariably die, then it is virtually impossible to argue that the declaration of civil war, in a cause that is sacred to those fighting it, is immoral. Terrorism is just that. And, given that there is only one human race, every war is a civil war.

If the aerial bombing of cities that kills thousands is now taken for granted as a normal way of waging war, or if at least five so-called civilised nations are prepared, in certain circumstances, to wage nuclear war, then to be outraged at the explosion of a car bomb, is strangely selective. Whatever others may think, to the terrorist who is as prepared to die as to kill, the cause will always be sacred. The difference is, the terrorist is not protected by the mystique of a uniform that constitutes a highly respected licence to kill. When, as in Northern Ireland, the terrorist is, if not loved, then at least respected by a substantial part of the community, then the distinction between terrorist and soldier virtually disappears. This becomes clear in those situations where one man's terrorist is another man's freedom fighter and the impartial outsider, unwilling to take sides, calls him a guerilla.

Zionist freedom fighters/terrorists helped to establish Israel in the teeth of British opposition. Arab freedom fighters/terrorists fight for Palestinian rights in the face of Zionist opposition. The IRA believes it is fighting a British occupying army and British people condemn it. The Maquis believed it was fighting a German occupying army and the British people helped it. President Reagan condemns terrorism/liberation struggle in El Salvador and finances it in Nicaragua. There is no end to such examples of selective indignation.

It is the worship of armed might, the unquestioning respect shown to military rank (what better example than the romantic, uniformed Prince at a royal wedding?) that gives the equally romantic terrorist his or indeed her moral justification. Father Richard McSoreley SJ, focusing this argument more narrowly on nuclear weapons, perhaps too narrowly, has written: 'The taproot of violence in our society today is our intent to use nuclear weapons. Once we have agreed to that, all other evil is minor in comparison. Until we squarely face the question of our consent to use nuclear weapons, any hope of large-scale improvement of public morality is doomed to failure.'

Terrorism, in the normal sense of that word, is virtually as old as human civilisation itself. If there are circumstances in which the improvement of the quality of life of many can only be achieved by the killing of others, and that is held to be moral, then there cannot be a blanket condemnation of terrorism. Whether a particular cause justifies it, will always be a matter of subjective judgement. To approve of the ANC is not necessarily to approve of the PLO or of the IRA.

Much more serious is the extension of the approval of killing to state sponsored killing, i.e. killing underwritten by whole nations, leading to the ultimate logic of producing weapons of mass destruction. Terrorists, unless they too acquire such weapons, do not threaten to end all life. That is still a state monopoly. Governments are now the greater threat. Militarism, taken to its logical conclusion, will either destroy what we know of civilisation, if not of creation, or, recognising the absurdity, will put an end to itself. It might then even be possible to start putting an end to terrorism, the lesser problem.

All this has been argued in an entirely secular way. It may well be, however, that having come close to the extinction of the human race, we will draw back and recognise that Jesus was simply ahead of his time in commending the principle of loving our enemies. Far from being wildly idealistic, it may be the only rational way to survive. To love our enemies and, in certain circumstances even to prefer defeat to war, may, in the future, be the only viable form of enlightened self-interest. The late Olof Palme's concept of 'common security' may come close to putting that in a usable political framework.

But let me not give the impression that the problem of defeating injustice and ending violence can be solved without suffering, without the cross. For me Gandhi's framework, though it may have Hindu roots, comes closest to the mind of Christ and could take us a little closer, pacifists and non-pacifists together, actually to achieving a just peace. 'To recognise evil and not to oppose it,' said Gandhi, 'is to surrender your humanity. To recognise evil and to oppose it with the weapons of the evil-doer is to enter into your humanity. To recognise evil and to oppose it with the weapons of God is to enter into your divinity.'

Gandhi does not condemn the soldier, or the freedom fighter/terrorist. But he points to a better way still. It is the way of the cross. Our prayer must be that the human family may yet be led to achieve its divine potential.

7

Kalinin Passion

Kalinin is a drab, industrial city on the long road from Leningrad to Moscow. It has few attractions for Western tourists. Yet I have reason – two reasons – to remember Kalinin as I remember no other place in the Soviet Union. They symbolise the cross in ways that could not be more different.

In my mid thirties, working as the East-West Relations Secretary of the British Council of Churches, I was chosen as joint leader of a party of young people on an exchange visit to the USSR, part of a scheme funded by the British and Soviet governments. From Tilbury docks we set sail on a Russian cruise ship. It was a holiday, but more than a holiday. It was for us all the kind of learning experience that never again makes it possible to see another nation in sloganising terms.

The pro-Soviet enthusiasts among us were made to think again, just as hard as the greater number who set out thinking they were quite brave to go to such a terrible country at all. To me it was not my first visit, but it was my first travelling, not as a professional churchman, but as just one more visitor. Yet it was my unadvertised priesthood that made my experience of Kalinin memorable.

At the end of the second of our Kalinin days I went off alone in the early evening to look for the Russian Orthodox church. I did not even know for sure whether there was one open, what the Russians call a working church. These were the days of Nikita Khrushchev who, though more liberal in most things than his Stalinist predecessors, was conducting a vigorous anti-religious campaign and closing down half the country's churches that had been reopened during and after what the Russians call the Great Patriotic War. Much of Kalinin had been fought over and destroyed. There were no prominent old churches to be seen anywhere.

My search took me right to the edge of the city. There I found the only working church. And despite my almost entire lack of Russian, I eventually, with much help from friendly people, found the priest's house, small, wooden, old and traditional. He appeared to have no family and spoke no English and very little German. But enough German for him to welcome me and ask me to wait. He returned with a woman who turned out to be the church's caretaker and who spoke German well. They were both probably in their fifties.

The long night that followed I shall never forget. Though a stranger, I was accepted with total openness as a fellow Christian and as an Anglican priest, though I had outward proof of neither. Father Pavel asked many questions over a long, though modest meal. Not, however, until with pride he had showed me his restored, though also modest church. He insisted that we should be photographed together on its steps.

Talking over the tomatoes, cucumbers, black bread and tea he then shared with me enough of his life and priesthood to open up for me the great and tragic panorama of the history of the Russian people over the last two generations. It is not a personal story to be retold. Many times he had lost everything, human and material, with only his inner resources to carry him through. And, like almost all priests of his generation, much of his life had been spent as a prisoner. He did not dramatise that or dwell on its suffering. He seemed simply grateful to have survived in body and soul. Of bitterness there was no trace. This was not an exceptional story. Many had suffered more in war and in almost equally terrible times of peace.

When we had prayed together and I got up to go he went to a cupboard, took out a box, and from the box took out a silver cross. It was the priest's cross he had received from the bishop at his ordination. He kissed me on both cheeks and hung it round my neck. He wanted me to have it, to take it back to England, to have it with me when I pray for the

Christians of Russia. It had, with him, survived Stalin's prison camps.

I hesitated to accept it. The tears it brought to my eyes made him insist the more that it was now mine. He smiled: 'I'm an archpriest now and wear a grander one.' It was to become for me, in the years that ensued, much more than another symbol of the suffering through which good triumphs over evil, it was the sign – a very beautiful one – of a unity that is both mystical and practical, personal and political and, at its centre, deeply loving, a unity that is already a reality in the heart of God. Jesus calls it the Kingdom. That cross to me, because of its history, because of the witness it had been, the martyrdom it had seen, was what the ecumenical movement is all about.

I wore it myself, very occasionally, after that. But my Western friends could not really grasp its meaning and my Orthodox friends, knowing very well what it was, were somewhat bewildered at my even possessing it. I began to think that God must have other plans for it, that it had not yet completed its pilgrimage.

A few years later another fellow priest, very far from Kalinin, was jailed. He and I had walked up Table Mountain together. He had shown me the beauty of the Cape. We had been followed, as we walked, by an agent of the South African Bureau of State Security. Now David Russell was a prisoner of apartheid. A mutual friend took the cross to him. It was back where it belonged, as the bond of the suffering Church which is a sign of hope in every place of fear and despair. I knew that Pavel and David were one, through the cross, in a worldwide sisterhood and brotherhood of faith, hope and love.

The word sisterhood compels me to add a postscript to that story. In most societies, to be self-effacing is held to be a feminine virtue, in Russia the sign of a woman's holiness. Yet is it not male domination that has effaced so much that women could and should have contributed? I had left the priest's house that night, much enriched by my experience. Hardly any of that would have been possible without the sensitive interpreting of a woman. She had been a gracious and willing servant. Only afterwards did this appear intolerable to me, for I have no doubt that she would have had a story to tell no less interesting and no less spiritually significant than Father Pavel's. He and I were the poorer for our insensitivity, just as the whole Church has long been the poorer for its unwillingness to let women take their rightful place in its life.

Which leads directly to the other reason that I shall not forget Kalinin. Her name was Katya. We were the guests of the Komsomol, the Young Communist League, the youth organisation that embraces almost all young Soviet people. Its leaders are generally over rather than under thirty. In each place our programme usually started with a social evening in a youth club, hosted and entertained by the Komsomol leaders in that place.

For the duration of our visit Katya had leave from her factory where she worked as a chemical engineer. She, with others, had been detailed to look after us well. She spoke some English. She was married to a Greek, one of many who had fled to the Soviet Union when the Communists were defeated in the late forties. He was, she told me, a constructional engineer working on a project in the Caucasus. They had no children.

I enjoyed Katya's company. She appeared to enjoy mine. She even seemed to cope with my appalling dancing. The thought of her as a companion and guide for the next four days made even a rather dreary city seem somewhat brighter. We had been saying all along, and said it in our welcoming speeches, that getting to know people mattered more to us than seeing places. Human relations before tourism. And there were plenty of spontaneous friendships springing up between our young people and some of their younger Komsomol hosts.

The relative liberality of the Khrushchev era made it all easier and more relaxed than in earlier – and indeed later – years. Visits to Russian homes were permitted and even encouraged. So it was that, on the third day, Katya invited me home and I readily accepted. I still have the beautifully painted wooden liqueur tumblers she gave me that day. Our relationship seemed easy, relaxed and unthreatening. I picked up no signals of the emotional storm that was brewing. Perhaps I had not read enough Russian novels to recognise the danger signals.

The last of our four days in Kalinin, a hot summer's day, was spent on an excursion by coach into the countryside, by boat on a river, finishing up to swim and sunbathe on a small sandy island. Still no signs of any problem until the final stretch back to Kalinin on the coach. In her halting English – even so, clearly and calmly – Katya informed me that there was no way she could go on living without me. I must stay with her in Kalinin. I chose to believe I had not heard right. But I had. Was this some kind of joke or, even worse, some kind of plot? It began to dawn on me that it was probably genuine. A kind of subdued passion for which I was totally unprepared emotionally and too bewildered to cope with practically.

My armoury was confined to calm reason, though I began to feel anything but calm. This situation would have been threatening anywhere. In Russia it felt like some kind of looming disaster. And something of the depth of feeling of a Dostoyevsky novel began to come through to me.

Beginning with my wife and children and going on to my obligations to the group I was leading, I finished up trying to convince Katya how the Soviet authorities would react. All of which, presumably, she already knew. It made no difference. About the only thing I didn't try, was to bring God into it.

By the time we were back in Kalinin, I seemed to have made some impression. I was definitely going on to Moscow the next morning. 'All right,' she said, 'if that's how you feel, I shall have to come with you.' I wrongly took that to be an empty threat. The danger had not passed. In the hotel the next morning, when we came down to breakfast, Katya was there, coat over her arm, a packed suitcase at her feet. I broke out in a sweat. Should I appeal for help to the Komsomol? That might cause immediate grave problems with the authorities, certainly for Katya. What about her work-place? Or was she perhaps in league with the authorities? Was this some kind of snare? I had an hour, before our coach was due to leave for Moscow. Breakfast didn't seem to matter any more.

To the not inconsiderable amusement of our young party I headed back up the stairs, with Katya in tow. Far from the light-hearted flirtation of their imaginings ('The Vicar and the Chemical Engineer' doesn't sound quite right anyway), my feet felt like lead. My room was small. The large bed almost filled it. Buddha-like, Katya sat, glaring, on the far corner of the bed, but with none of the Buddha's serenity. More like a smouldering volcano.

Could I persuade her? What was open to me, verbally or non-verbally, bearing in mind how limited her English was and how non-existent my Russian? Nothing seemed to make any difference. Was my monologue even half understood? I no longer thought it possible that this could all be some kind of act. This really was passion of a kind I had only read about. Even had it not been outside my emotional range, to have made any kind of positive response would have been to court disaster. I fell back on conventional arguments, not from love of convention, for this was no conventional situation, but because my options seemed to be so limited.

In the end there was just silence. I had almost given up hoping for any kind of resolution. God, at such critical moments, seems particularly inaccessible. Even so, I probably prayed, in a kind of way. I don't even quite know what it was I feared.

The drama ended (melodrama?) even more surprisingly than it had begun. Had this been an American B film, a pistol and a double killing, murder and suicide, might have ended it all. But as the ideology demands, I imagine Soviet stories all have to be positively resolved. And, in a fashion, this one was.

As though, having been blind, she could suddenly see, Katya visibly changed. All she had left for me now was anger and disdain, more than enough to rescue her self-esteem. Her back now to the door, straight and tense, she almost spat the words at me that resolved the issue for her: 'You are no man. You are priest.' She picked up her suitcase, slammed the door behind her, and was gone.

Passion literally means suffering. It is no accident that the word usually has either religious or sexual significance. There is a deep underlying relationship between the two. It is strongly present in classical, pre-revolutionary Russian literature. It is a recurrent theme in the novels of Graham Greene. Indeed it has been said that if politics is added to religion and sexuality, the whole of life has been encompassed.

This short-lived Kalinin passion was no doubt very Russian in its atmosphere and intensity. My descriptive powers certainly fail to do it justice. (If it was other than a spontaneous expression of human emotion, if it were some kind of act, then Katya had missed out on a potentially brilliant stage career.) However, what makes me tell the story here alongside that of Father Boris is that I believe it has significance far beyond its Russian setting. And it is also about the cross. Another cross that the Church has inflicted on the world.

Both historically and in the present, the Churches' failure to root their understanding of sexuality in the openness, the sensitivity, the forgiveness and the compassion of Christ is rivalled only by their failure (like Jerusalem's) to comprehend what truly makes for peace.

The intuitive knowledge of that came to Katya's rescue when she needed a way of escape. For a moment good came of something which was anything but good. Speaking theological shorthand, traditional moral theology, running right through the greater part of 'mainline Christianity', has left sexuality firmly in the grip of the law. Freedom has been too threatening to allow the gospel to recreate a new vision of human relationships at their deepest level. Roman Catholic canon law is the most clear outward and visible sign of what I mean. Eastern Orthodox and Western Protestant traditions are sufficiently similar to make the distinctions insignificant. Legalistic thinking on marriage, celibacy, priesthood and ministry, procreation, homosexuality and much more have left generation after generation in emotional chains. That this has been tempered in numerous ways by pastoral sensitivity does not touch the core of the case against what most people would simply call 'the Christian religion'.

Katya, knowing that I was a priest (though it had not explicitly featured in our all too brief relationship), was, in the end, able to associate priesthood with the death of sexuality. And so to un-man me. It was the ultimate human put-down. It was, more than she had probably realised, a remarkable moment of truth. A judgement worthy to be recorded.

It has become deeply, culturally embedded in Christian civilisation that there is a conflict between religion and the physical expression of love. I can remember a long and earnest discussion with my fiancée whether, when I was wearing my cassock, the outward sign of my religious commitment, it would be proper for us to be seen holding hands. Ridiculously trivial as that now seems, that was the proverbial tip of an iceberg, that has often managed to freeze the Christian religion to the bone.

I studied, and so may have some technical knowledge of, politics. I feel competent to say that the Marxist critique of religion in general and of the Christian religion in particular is largely justified. Yet at no point does it even begin to shake my faith in Christ crucified and risen. That is because there is a dialectical relationship – in other words antagonism – between the Church and its Lord. Or, in more popular language, between Churchianity and Christianity.

If that is true in the realm I partly understand, all my instincts tell me that it is at least as true in a realm I understand less well. I am no psychologist. Even so, my personal and my pastoral experience has taught me that it is not necessary to worship Freud to recognise that many human beings have, through centuries, been emotionally enslaved by a wrong, disincarnate reading of Christ. God, robbed of his flesh-and-blood humanity. But God, as the American satirist E. Y. Harburg suggests, certainly keeps his own options open, for:

When lightening struck the steeple
Of the Church at San José
It barely missed the brothel
That was just across the way.

I would rather then be the morally dissolute priest of Graham Greene fiction, reliant entirely on Christ's compassion and in no kind of doubt that I was part and parcel of a fallen world, crying out for a Saviour, than the 'eunuch of Kalinin'. But those are not the real choices. Promiscuity (of many kinds) and puritanism (of an equally wide variety) are simply two alternative forms of captivity. Though in many ways pained by its frigidity, I am not surprised at the conservative backlash against the uncaring hedonism of the sixties which sometimes posed as a kind of Christian liberation. If 'anything goes', nothing, in the end, has deeper meaning and all relationships become trivial. Love itself ceases to have meaning. Let no one then interpret my Kalinin experience as leading to a plea for that kind of unloving permissiveness. Love will always be costly. Ecstasy and agony cannot be torn apart. Passion will always also mean suffering.

But there is a divine kind of permissiveness which must somehow become part of a reborn Christendom. If canon law that even remotely resembles what it is now, remains the touch-stone of what the Church has to say about human relationships, all it will do is to give shelter to those who want protection from themselves and their fellow human beings. The law, for those who want it, can provide a kind of security. That is not to be despised. In Britain today, Mary Whitehouse and the many for whom she speaks, deserve to be taken a lot more seriously than most *Guardian* readers could understand. But to walk with Jesus and with the strong women who were his friends is to choose a freedom that is vulnerable and insecure and mysterious and certainly not containable in a book of canon law. It is, knowing that we are loved, setting out to discover the meaning of the glorious liberty of the children of God. Again, the Bird of Heaven must be allowed to fly.

So, more painful as that might have been, I wish I had not been rescued in Kalinin by my priesthood.

8

Nazareth

Every Christian who is persuaded to sign up for a 'pilgrimage to the Holy Land' should be given a form to fill in. The first question should read: 'Why do you seek the living among the dead?' It is the question the women, who were Jesus' closest friends, were asked when they came with spices to his tomb.

Ever since that day Christians have proclaimed and celebrated the resurrection of Jesus. It was a mystery then, it remains a mystery now. The life of the Church depends on its truth. So earth-shattering, so profound is that truth that any attempt to reduce it to doctrinal definition or simply to a historical event is bound to belittle its significance. None of the biblical narratives do more than point with awe to the mystery.

The tragedy of Christian history is that the Churches have, by and large, put the risen Christ in a new set of ecclesiastical tombs. To suggest, as David Jenkins, the Bishop of Durham, does, that such a doctrine cannot be enshrined in definitions that satisfy pedestrian reason, that it cannot be reduced to historical statements, is not to sabotage the Church's mission but to breathe life into it. It is, however, to sabotage faith in the gilded places of pilgrimage, in the rococo Church which insists on putting Christ, spiced and embalmed, on golden thrones; insists on making him our kind of King. That Christ is no more than a triumphal tribal deity. He is as dead, defunct, deceased as the parrot in a celebrated comedy act of British television. Not surprisingly it is necessary to shout very loud that he is alive, because there is no sign of his life in his worshippers.

I do not quite want to suggest that a new Wilberforce is

needed to conduct a campaign against the pilgrimage trade to Israel. The only people who are harmed are the pilgrims who, unlike the slaves, freely choose to be. I have no wish to see Israeli and Palestinian tour operators and guides done out of their livelihood or even clerics, who offer to lead such journeys, out of a free holiday. But at least a warning might be written into the glossy brochures: 'This tour may damage your spiritual health.'

To begin with, to call any one country 'the Holy Land' is, inevitably, to suggest that in some way the rest of God's creation is less holy. The fact that salvation history, as Christians understand it, largely happened in and around the countries of the eastern Mediterranean is, of course, of genuine interest. It even, given our justified love of scripture, has very real sentimental significance. Let it not be thought that I object to tourism that takes account of that. But genuine pilgrimage is something very different. It is not religious archaeology. It demands an answer to the question: 'Why do you seek the living among the dead?'

I fear the answer is very painful. Too many of us prefer our religion in historic wrappings, in ancient creeds, bound in calf leather. That way it cannot get under our skin. It will leave us in the complacent knowledge that our faith cannot be shaken and that our God is the same yesterday, today and for ever. But is he?

A really living Christ is far too threatening and so is a Holy Spirit who doesn't only live in rousing pentecostal choruses.

The poets are far closer to reality, and some of our hymn writers too. They point us to genuine pilgrimage, to resurrection at the end of a road of many crosses:

We hear thy cry of anguish, we see thy life outpoured,
Where battlefield runs red with blood, our brother's blood,
   O Lord.
And in that bloodless battle, the fight for daily bread,
Where might is right and self is king, we see thy thorn-
   crowned head.

The groaning of creation, wrung out of pain and care,
The anguish of a million hearts that break in dumb despair;
O crucified Redeemer, these are thy cries of pain;
O may they break our selfish hearts and love come in to
    reign.

(Timothy Rees)

The wonder is, of course, and the proof of the resurrection,
that Christ cannot be held in gilded ecclesiastical chains. The
prophets and saints and martyrs of every age are living
witnesses to the resurrection. Again and again the stone, the
heavy weight of religion, is rolled away and the Lord of life
escapes from the cathedrals built to contain him and goes on,
unrecognised as on the road to Emmaus, washing feet. He will
even, still unrecognised, return to where those who bear his
name are gathered and will offer to share his life with them.
We may reduce our meetings for worship and our eucharistic
liturgies to divisive ceremonies and sectarian rites. He keeps
faith: 'Where two or three are gathered together in my name,
there am I in the midst.'

It is this Christ of whom Sydney Carter makes us sing:

They cut me down and I leap up high;
I am the life that will never, never die;
I'll live in you if you'll live in me:
I am the Lord of the dance, said he.

He will lead us a merry dance, if we let him. There is a way
to meet him in our family, in our street, in our friends and in
our enemies. And in ourselves. The Holy Land is always on
our doorstep. Every day can be a pilgrimage – if that's what
we want. There is no initial fee but, like the rich young ruler,
we may find the real cost is more than we are willing to pay.

Having taken the health warning into account, the cruise
ship to Palestine remains an option. One of the most
uncomfortable and intelligent Christians I have known, Stanley
Evans, whom I once served as curate, was actually persuaded
by his bishop to join such a pilgrimage party. He published his

diary of the experience and called it *In Evening Dress to Calvary*. He went on the kind of principle that one packet of Balkan Sobranies is not likely to give you lung cancer. So, take the risk if you will!

Now let me be more constructive. There are many worthwhile places for Christians, who can afford it, to visit. None more than Israel and occupied Palestine. In an extraordinary way it does reflect the situation in which Jesus lived. It manages to be a microcosm of our embittered and embattled world. Some even think that if another world war were to break out, this is where it would start. It remains a land of many crosses.

Christian pilgrimage in that turbulent, alienated setting means a period of immersion in the lives of the people today. That means sharing their hopes and fears, their triumphs and their suffering. It means eating with them and praying with them. It means listening and learning and caring. It is possible. Some have done it. Weddings still happen in Cana. Fishermen still go out on the Sea of Galilee. Tears are still shed over a Jerusalem that does not know the things that make for peace, and prophets are still thrown out of Nazareth. Bethlehem is still under foreign occupation. In that context, the need to watch and pray with Jesus in the Garden of Gethsemane is as great as it was two thousand years ago.

Where else in the world is the religious tragedy more evident? In a very small area Jews and Moslems and Christians, each, in their own way, declaring this to be *their* Holy Land, live unreconciled lives. They claim, in their different ways, to worship the same God. Yet the same God keeps them apart. Daily, Israeli Jews and Palestinian Arabs live and die in fear of each other. And in Jerusalem there is the awe-inspiring memorial to six million Jews, murdered in our lifetime by what called itself a Christian nation. What better place for a pilgrimage of penitence? That memorial is a more important station of the cross today than the place where it is thought that Jesus died. But more important still are the refugee camps on the West Bank where Jesus is suffering now. And the homes of Jews, rejected by many of their fellow Israelis, because they say no to Zionist racism and want to live on terms of equality with their Arab neighbours.

And what kind of pilgrimage is it that prays our Western prayers, celebrates our Western eucharists, thinks our Western thoughts and passes by the Eastern churches that have lived and prayed and suffered here for centuries? A passing nod to them, a fleeting moment in their churches, an accepted cup of coffee does not answer that question. They are deeply hurt by the pilgrimage industry in its present form. Their poverty and their graciousness hide that from most visitors.

What better place than the lands of the eastern Mediterranean today to reflect penitently on the price the world is asked to pay for the quarrels and feuds between believers in God? Not only are Christians, Moslems and Jews unreconciled with each other, they are deeply divided within themselves. Even in the face of a common enemy orthodox Jews find it impossible to live in harmony with their unorthodox fellow Jews. Even in the face of a common enemy bitter feuds divide Moslem from Moslem. Even in the age of the ecumenical movement, and as an often embattled minority in the Middle East, there are still many Christians who will not talk to their fellow Christians.

All this is the real world. And in that world, most wonderfully, signs of the resurrection, love triumphing over evil, are to be found. There may, somewhere, be the empty tomb of history. What does it matter, when the Lord of history is alive in the back streets of Nazareth and the high rise blocks of Tel Aviv now?

I went there for the first time in 1963, alone, simply to 'discover Israel'. I had a few addresses with me. They led to others: Jewish, Moslem and Christian. I slept only one night in a hotel. I seldom drove alone in my little hired car. The people and their hopes and fears came alive for me. Nazareth was my base. A Scottish doctor, serving the local Arabs, my initial host.

Nazareth is Israel's largest Arab town. It reflects most of its problems. The population, mainly poor Arabs, had a communist mayor. Egypt's Nasser was then their hero. In Israel all these Arabs were made to feel like second-class citizens in their own land. And the Jews feared and distrusted these Arabs. They were a security risk, so a new Jewish Nazareth was being built on the hilltops, overlooking the old town.

Where, in the midst of all this, was the most conspicuous Christian presence? In the heart of the town a great basilica was under construction, nearly completed. The Franciscan guardians of the holy places were its architects and builders. Who was it for? Not the local Arab Christians. To them it was a Western import of no spiritual significance. To the Moslems it merely outrivalled their mosques. It was there, a friar from the American midwest told me, to the glory of God and for the inspiration of visiting Christians.

I did not have the heart to say to the friar that, in that situation, St Francis would have pulled that place down with his own hands. Here was an irrelevant, triumphalist church that seemed to contradict everything that Jesus the Carpenter stands for. With great sadness my Scottish host told me how many millions of dollars the basilica was costing, while a very much smaller amount required to complete a much needed old people's home a stone's throw from the basilica could not be found. Of Christ the worker, the reconciler, the liberator, this edifice had nothing to say. It was – as is so much of the life of organised religion – an anti-sacrament. The one redeeming factor was that most local Christians seemed to feel that way about it.

Arab Nazareth in an Israeli state and with this kind of Christian presence left me asking, in a biblical phrase: 'Can anything good come out of Nazareth?'

I was assured, it can. My question was anticipated. My presbyterian host took me down a hillside, into a valley, up a steep path. As we walked he told me part of the story of the man he was taking me to meet. Father Paul Gauthier had been the head of a Roman Catholic seminary in the South of France. He had come as a pilgrim to Israel and been so shocked by the experience that, after long and agonised prayer, he asked leave of his bishop to resign from teaching theology and to go to Palestine in the hope that God would show him a way to serve that would be an alternative Christian presence there. So he went.

He arrived with no blueprint. Only two things were clear to him. The two communities, Jewish and Arab, would need to accept him. Only on those terms was Christian service possible. That meant getting to know both communities, their language and their customs. And that would take years. He started with the Arabs who agreed to take him on as a building labourer in and around Nazareth.

Climbing up the steep path, we came to a narrow cave entrance. My guide knew that at this hour, in the early evening, Father Paul would be there. This was his church. Here in about an hour the eucharist would be celebrated. A wiry figure with strong sinewy hands and warm penetrating eyes welcomed us. The cave was large enough to hold about twenty people, standing shoulder to shoulder. It was white, bright and spotless. A simple wooden table in the middle. We sat down, Arab fashion, on the floor. There was time to talk, time for Paul Gauthier to tell me his own story.

It was published around that time as *Nazareth Diary* by Geoffrey Chapman in English translation. Of that early period Paul Gauthier wrote:

> To become a worker with the workers, to work alongside them and like them, to live as far as possible like them, this is the aim of the worker apostolate. Without this, there would be no love. To act otherwise would be to take the wrong road . . . in relation to Jesus the poor man. This impression of having taken the wrong road is experienced painfully by some of the priests and religious here. One of them told me in his distress:
>
> > From the missionary point of view, we have taken the wrong road here. We live our lives on the fringe of the lives of the poor. We have large houses to live in while they have nowhere to live. We can hardly speak their

language . . . They see us as foreigners, protected and subsidised by foreign nations. We are divided among ourselves. The different rites criticise and distrust one another. Yes, we have taken the wrong turning, through our lack of poverty and charity.

Jesus became man and lived among us right here on earth, like any ordinary Jew in this village, like any workman, living, eating and toiling like a poor man, out of love. He gave the following missionary instructions to his apostles: 'I send you out as lambs in the midst of wolves . . . carry no purse, no bag, no sandals. Eat what is set before you . . . Say to them: "The Kingdom of God has come near to you." '

In simple, lucid French Father Gauthier spoke of his affection for the Arab working people among whom he lived during what he described as his 'long retreat'. And he spoke of his anger at the way they were exploited. The contractors gave no thought to the workers' conditions or their health. Only profits mattered. On this he commented in his diary: 'Even on this small site, Leo XIII's saying, which on this point agrees with Karl Marx, has a terrible ring of truth about it: "Matter is ennobled, man is degraded." This is modern society's answer to Jesus' question: "What does it profit a man if he gain the whole world, but suffers the loss of his own soul?" Man gains the whole world by exploiting man. He loses his soul twice over: by making himself a slave to money and technology and by exploiting his fellow men . . . Why then be surprised that communism finds such keen followers in Nazareth?'

The 'long retreat' as an Arab worker was followed by another. This time as a worker on a Jewish kibbutz. Again, without any priestly privileges. He could not have understood the common people, had he not dispensed with those. 'I had never been treated roughly on a train because I was wearing dungarees, or sent out of a church, or unable to board the trolley-bus because I was penniless, nor had I been without food, or without shelter for the night. All these things had come my way only when I put off my cassock, gave up my

Citroen and duties and post as a seminary professor to be just
a priest and, outwardly, a workman.'

When the mornings and evenings of prayer and the days of
work – the long retreat – were over, after a short period back
in France, Paul Gauthier knew what his vocation was to be.
He returned to Nazareth to pray – hence his cave-church in
the hillside – and, having won the confidence and cooperation
of a group of Jews and Arabs, to build a cooperative housing
settlement for some of the poorest, homeless Arab families.
By the time I arrived in Nazareth the houses had been built on
the hillside above the chapel. I had seen the children, happily
playing around them. Much more such work waited to be done.

We had been sitting, talking, for almost an hour. Gradually
more people came and sat down around us. It was time for the
liturgy. This was the Middle East, it was an Eastern rite that
Father Gauthier used. That of the Melchite community. The
group that gathered could not have been more varied. No one
asked to what nation, race, class or religious rite she or he
belonged. The bread was broken, the wine poured out for
the whole divinely human family. There was an integral unity
between this eucharist and the housing settlement on the hill
above as there was an integral unity between this eucharist and
the Last Supper of the Lord of the eucharist. Here earth and
heaven, time and eternity became one. All the paradoxes and
contradictions of life were resolved. I understood better than
before what Jesus must have meant when he said: 'the Kingdom
of God is very near.' Of that celebration of life, risen life, I
can say now: if that had been the only eucharist I ever shared
in, it would have sufficed.

As we came out of the cave the sun was setting. I had a final
question that related not only to this liturgy but to the life and
work and prayer of which it was evidently the heart. 'Is this,'
I said, pointing both to the cave and the settlement around it,
'is this what you mean by mission? Is this how you bring Jesus
to the people?' A look of pity greeted my question. Almost as
though he wished he had misunderstood me. 'Brother,' he said,
in French of such simplicity and clarity that I could not have

misunderstood, 'I have not brought Christ to these people. Because, in their love, they allow me to meet some of their needs, every new day I rediscover Christ in them.'

Twenty years later I ask myself whether I have begun to learn that lesson. Individually we are often as slow to learn from experience as communities and nations – and as the Church. Father Gauthier's diaries reveal that what shocked him deeply in the fifties had been written by Sir Frederick Treves in *The Land of Desolation* in 1912: 'If a hundreth part of the money allocated to the religious budget of Nazareth had been spent in improving the condition of the poor, there would be more happiness in Nazareth than there is at present. The contrast between the fine convents and monasteries, built of good stone, and the filthy hovels that surround them is a striking anomaly. When the Christians of Nazareth, having exhausted all the possibilities of pomp and magnificence, condescend to humble themselves to the level of the homes of the poor, it will be a good thing for the place, because then perhaps the teaching of him who was gentle and poor will reach the lives of the people.'

This is as true now as it was in 1912. It is as true in New York and London and Belfast and Liverpool as it is in Nazareth. It is true of me. 'Clothed in fine raiment' and housed better than most people, I wonder, is it still possible to be in a state of grace as a dignitary (*sic!*) of Coventry – or indeed any other – Cathedral of the Church of England? If the answer is yes, then the word grace is the only explanatory clue.

That is really what *Faith in the City*, that critical and self-critical report of and to the Church of England, is all about. Will its message be heard and heeded by more than a handful of Christians? How many of us could sing with William Blake – without the words sticking in our throat?

I will not cease from mental fight,
Nor shall my sword sleep in my hand,
Till we have built Jerusalem
In England's green and pleasant land.

Today Blake's words sound like the ultimate irony. Jerusalem?
Don't we have enough troubles in Britain without wanting to
import Jerusalem's? Can Christians do no better than produce
symbols that only underline the impossibility of the Jewish
dream of *shalom*, or its secularised version, Marx's 'scientific'
dream of communism, or its Christian version, Jesus' procla-
mation of the coming Kingdom?

Any ideologist or fundamentalist who dismisses that sceptical
question as faithless is like the man who says: 'Don't confuse
me with the facts.' He is a fool. I hope I am not an ideologist.
I hope I am not a fundamentalist in liberal disguise. Yet 'the
love that will not let me go' says to me: 'You will have to risk
being that kind of fool.' For Christ's sake. If even one Paul
Gauthier remains I shall be able to go on believing with Paul
the Apostle that 'neither death nor life, nor angels nor principalities, nor things present nor things to come, nor height, nor
depth, nor anything else in all creation, will be able to separate
us from the love of God'.

There are other Gauthiers to be visited in Israel today. There
are communities and individuals struggling for justice and
reconciliation. For *shalom*. There are public and, no doubt,
hidden places of possible pilgrimage. But all that despite and
not because of the realities of power. Paul Gauthier himself
did not survive among the Jews and Arabs he loved. His
demand for justice for the Palestinian people was more than
the Israeli authorities could live with. It had been his dream to
do in Bethlehem, in occupied Palestine, what he had begun to
do in Nazareth. Instead he was expelled from Israel. Works of
mercy, the kind of compassion shown by Mother Teresa and
her Sisters, the Caesars of this world can live with. But not the
works of mercy that begin to judge Caesar. Such was Paul
Gauthier's work. Such had taken Jesus to the judgement hall
and beyond.

It is to Paul Gauthier that I owe the somewhat enigmatic
title of this book. The double cross has as many meanings as
the reader chooses to give it. There is surely the occasional
inescapable question whether God – if there really is a God –

is not playing a fast one on us all. Or the author on his readers. Among the many other possibilities there is the definition of a Jew that stems from Nathan the sculptor, one of Paul Gauthier's Jewish friends: 'A Jew is someone who bears the cross without Christ.' Many in our world do that. And not seldom the cross is imposed on them by those who call themselves Christian but have reduced their own cross to a harmless ornament.

Paul Gauthier tells in his diary of a Jewish audience he addressed in Haifa where he shared Nathan the sculptor's definition of a Jew and also Bishop Fulton Sheen's dictum that 'the East has taken the cross without Christ, whereas the West has taken Christ but without His cross'. At the end of his address an elderly worker asked Father Gauthier: 'Are you prepared to be crucified?' The diary tells us: 'He had suffered in his life. He had carried his cross without Christ. He had a right to enquire whether we Christians, who live on Christ, are ready to follow our Master to the end.'

We who are Christians have no right to ask Jews anything. That has been forfeited long ago. But if real pilgrimage is our intent, if the stations of the cross are the goal of our journey, then does love not compel us to ask our Jewish sisters and brothers in Israel: 'Where is your journey leading? Can you not hear the Prophet Micah declaring that the Lord requires only this, that you do justice, love, kindness and walk humbly with your God? Are not you, whose kinsfolk the *Herrenvolk* killed, now playing the master race in your own land? Are not you who have suffered so long at Christian hands exacting punishment of those who have not wronged you? Have you not hardened your hearts against your Palestinian sisters and brothers, bringing upon your children and children's children the holocaust from which you were saved?'

Those who dare ask such questions need not fear. They have not come seeking the living among the dead. They have heard the voice of Moses saying: 'I have set before you life and death, blessing and curse; therefore choose life that you and your children may live.'

9

Getting Done Over

Robin Day inspires confidence. He is often better briefed than those in authority. If some 'act of God' or, more likely, of evil men were, at one stroke, to wipe out all of Britain's political leaders, the people – unless it's true that the British always prefer amateurs – might well be ready to place their destiny in Sir Robin's hands. He came up through the BBC the long hard way. To interview people with authority, sensitivity and tenacity is both an art and a craft. It calls for something of the humanity of the skilled priest whose task, even in the confessional, is to make the penitent want to tell the truth, but never to strip him naked. If the penitent *chooses* to reveal all, that does not rob him of his human dignity. If the impenitent politician prevaricates like Harold Wilson or blusters like Margaret Thatcher, the interviewer has really won anyway.

Media success goes to the head. It is not surprising that not a few potential government ministers have preferred to present history being made rather than to help make it; except that in some areas of life, the media really is the message. You don't even have to look like a character out of Dallas, though it probably helps a little. Certainly, as Robert Kilroy-Silk has found, politics demands enormous stamina. But so, as he will find, does television. It is not a soft option. It can even be a caring profession.

Stemming from my own days as a BBC producer, my anger is easily aroused when people are simply used and abused as media fodder. My sensitivity-training in this field I owe largely to Leslie Smith whom some old BBC Home Service listeners will remember. In early years a colleague of Robin Day, he enabled people to share both joy and suffering in the kind of humane yet penetrating interviews that the merchants of our tabloid press would not even have an ear to hear. The way the mass circulation papers feed, vampire-like, on human weakness and depravity, overlaid with sickly sentimentality and prurient morality, poses questions to our society as grave as those posed to Soviet society by the censored sterility of *Pravda* and *Izvestia*.

It was my fortune, I cannot make up my mind whether good or bad, to be the statutory parson, the 'voice of religion', in the pilot programme of the current affairs series to be presented by Robert Kilroy-Silk. He may even let that experiment be shown one day as part of a comic series featuring 'disasters the public never saw'. Its subject was nudity. A large audience was present to discuss its pros and cons. I doubt if even the most sensitive and experienced of presenters could have coped with the feelings and passions that were aroused. That hour confirmed my feeling that this is a subject British society cannot handle. It is still trapped between the false alternatives of the repressed sexuality of Victorian England and the unbridled permissiveness that is the other side of the same coin. Neither have any moral credibility.

The very word nudity has overtones in English that its French original quite lacks. Nakedness is a little easier to handle. The matter is one of culture. To even discuss nakedness in an Islamic setting would be grossly insensitive. As insensitive as colonising missionaries forcing native peoples to cover their nakedness with Victorian finery. Clearly in a culturally pluralist and mixed society, as Britain is today, there is a problem. It deserves discussion. Like every serious subject, it also has its funny side. Part of the problem is that neither those who earnestly defend nudity nor those who find it utterly offensive are inclined to laugh about it. And the many who do not take sides are mildly embarrassed, as their mind moves to dirty seaside postcards. Which is exactly what had happened to the producers of this BBC pilot programme. To 'lighten' it, they suddenly produced, in the midst of emotional heat, three naked male characters from a comic programme, only just hiding their genitals with various suggestively shaped balloons.

In shocked horror, the opponents of nudity walked off the television set. They had been deeply offended. The defenders of nudity as something natural did not know what to do. They should have been equally offended, for this was not nudity but prudish and prurient farce. The pilot programme did not recover after that. All that was left for the BBC to do was apologise to all concerned and maybe learn a lesson. The moral issue that should have been discussed is the increasing use of the female body for commercial sexploitation. Here, to their mutual embarrassment, the women's movement and the neo-puritans now find themselves in the same lobby. The borderline between life-enhancing eroticism and degrading exploitation remains undefined, while the continuing treatment of women as male commodities remains a social scandal. These are matters the TV pilot programme hardly touched on.

If naked communal bathing were as natural to the British as to many Japanese and Germans, from the very young to the very old, nudity would soon cease to be a matter for debate. It happens that my wife and I are heirs to that tradition, which perhaps explains my presence in the TV studio that crazy Sunday afternoon. A recent West German TV documentary on the life of an East German Lutheran pastor and his family began on a sandy Baltic beach where all the family and most of the other bathers were naked. It raised no eyebrows on either side of the Berlin Wall. In the cold winters, when the beaches are empty, virtually every village has its welcoming family sauna where, for a few hours at least, there is something like the classless society. Anything less like the sleazy image invoked for some in Britain by the word sauna is hard to imagine.

Given our love for this healthy Finnish pastime and our dislike of being segregated, my wife and I discovered a club in the West End of London which made it possible to recapture some of the relaxation of our German holidays . . . though necessarily rather more privately. Nothing quite like the fun of the hundreds of families spending a summer's day in the saunas, pools and on the spacious lawns of our favourite German baths near Frankfurt, built in Japanese style and at a price even those on the dole can afford. Being a London club, its licence needed to be renewed, year by year. Its respectability needed to be vouched for to the Royal Borough of Kensington and Chelsea by 'worthy' people like parsons and doctors and judges. One year, I was asked to write an appropriate letter – and did. The consequences were sadly and amusingly British.

A journalist from a Sunday newspaper that thrives on sex, scandal, grief and crime rang up with a question that set all my alarm bells ringing: 'Vicar, is it correct that you belong to a nudist club? We believe you've commended it for a new licence.' 'My wife and I,' I replied, 'enjoy sauna bathing. It isn't done to wear clothes in a sauna. Yes, I did commend our club.'

The young reporter was fascinated. He thought he was on to a big story and asked, could he come, with a photographer, to interview us. 'Of course you can,' I said, 'but you've already had the whole story. That's all there is to tell.' They came. There was as little to say as I'd warned, but even so, the two departed, well satisfied. It wasn't difficult to imagine the titillating article and the kind of headlines that a little journalistic invention would produce. Here was the other side of the 'free press', free to cause embarrassment, confusion and pain to helpless, unsuspecting people. What a scoop, a sexy story about a political parson! That combines just about everything.

This parson wasn't helpless. His anger was for the many people who don't know how to protect themselves. I simply rang the editor and, in the friendliest possible way, told him that if a misleading, damaging article appeared I'd go straight to the Press Council.

I've retold that story (and will not forget its sequel) as an interesting curtain raiser to a far more important story in the life of my south east London parish. It is the story of how a Christian community that tried to be open to the needs of people who don't belong to the Church encountered and then fought the racism that is so deeply rooted in our social structures. I retell the tale that happened in the early seventies because it has since become clear that it is far more typical than most people are prepared to admit. Much pain continues to be borne by immigrant minorities and most of the nation is hardly aware of it.

The Quaye family lived opposite the curate's house in the parish. Bill, who worked for British Rail, had come to Britain from Ghana and married Ellen, a native Londoner. They had two attractive black daughters, Kathleen 19 and Susan 17. They were a friendly, articulate, outgoing family. Like many a teenager, Susan had had some minor brushes with the law, quite a problem for her strict law-abiding parents. One night Mum and Dad and Kathleen knocked at the vicarage door. They wanted me to know that Susan had been picked up by the Greenwich police after a fight in the park. Her three white friends had got away. Susan was being held on suspicion of making off with another girl's purse. Two policewomen had come to the flat to search it, but they had no warrant, so Bill had sent them away. Now the family were going down to the Station to see Susan. There, a racially abusive detective sergeant met them, told them they could not see Susan and finished by telling them: 'I'm going to turn you over as you've never been turned over before.'

The Quayes began their half-hour walk home. When they got near the house they found it surrounded by squad cars, about six, and anything up to twenty uniformed and plain clothes police. Frightened, Bill Quaye made for the curate's house opposite, wanting some witnesses to what was happening. At the front door he was forcibly dragged away, back across the street to his own house, with the police all round him. He tried to free himself but failed. His wife and daughter came to his aid. He struggled hard and was there upon arrested and charged with attempted unlawful and malicious grievous bodily harm, and the two women with assault. All were taken to the Station. The flat was searched and nothing incriminating found.

At the Station Bill was further abused, and left naked in his cell for over an hour. Later in the night I went down and bailed out the three women. The next day the whole family appeared in court and were remanded; Susan to Holloway Prison. Kathleen claimed she too had been racially abused and had had her face slapped.

When the case came to trial Susan was acquitted of theft but put on probation for her part in the fight, though none of the others involved were arrested. The serious charge against Bill was dropped as soon as it was challenged, but he, his wife and his daughter were all convicted of assault. The detective sergeant and the many other officers had carefully coordinated their evidence. The magistrate commented that this was one of the most unfortunate cases he had had to try. He imposed only the most nominal sentences. Even so, the whole family now had a record. They had been successfully victimised.

There was no doubt in our Parish Council. We would stand by the family, hire an experienced civil rights lawyer and see the case through to appeal. In the Crown Court it all looked very different. An old lady who had witnessed the scene and who had two sons in the police was listened to with care. What she had seen did not tally with the police evidence, it did with the family's. Mr and Mrs Quaye gave evidence and, said the judge, 'we have been impressed throughout this case by the demeanor of the appellants and we were also impressed by the evidence which they gave and the way they gave it. We were impressed by the way they stood up to cross-examination'. He found no case had been proved against father, mother or daughter. The family had been cleared.

The police ordered an official enquiry into the whole case, as a result of which the detective sergeant left the police force. What does all this amount to? That it is possible, but not easy, to get justice. It does not justify the cry of 'pigs' whenever police appear on the scene. One senior officer who is corrupt and prejudiced can wreck the reputation of the whole Station. Did our parish intervention wreck our relationship with the local police? Far from it. Some of the younger officers who had been knelt on to tell lies quietly thanked us.

If there is at least some truth in the assertion that the Church exists for the benefit of those who are not its members, then the Quaye case is a good illustration of what such openness implies. Solidarity with this mixed-race family was in no way in conflict with solidarity of a critical kind with the forces of law and order. Both the Quayes and the police were helped, in the end. That this sort of commitment, widely known through press reporting, was part of the local Church's mission and of its witness to the wider community, was an extra bonus. That there would be an even more demanding sequel, none of us expected.

Now I must return to the early part of this chapter. The news of the successful Quaye appeal was followed within days by the arrival at our vicarage of the Sunday paper journalists looking for their scoop about the vicar and the sauna. There was, of course, no connection. Having fired a shot across the editor's bow, I was not much worried about a salacious story. Even so, come Sunday, after the early Communion, I walked to the newsagent and surprised him by my additional choice of paper that morning. My guess was justified. At the bottom of an inside page there was a one-and-a-half-inch story of the Blackheath vicar who had commended a sauna club to the Royal Borough of Kensington and Chelsea. Factual, harmless and utterly uninteresting.

In good spirits I returned to the vicarage to share the news with my wife. At the gate, good spirits turned to near panic. Parked outside were four cars, each filled with people reading the papers. My rapid conclusion: this story is only just starting. Here now are the tabloid dailies, waiting to appear at our morning service, waiting to ask loaded questions and to take pictures. A gloomy breakfast, with every expectation of the kind of media torment to which so many people are subjected day by day. The best I could think of was that even this might make it possible to communicate something about our open church and the love of God for all people. If others had to face this, why shouldn't we? So, squaring up to the inevitable, I gathered my courage to cross the road to the church opposite.

What faced me was utterly unexpected and totally welcome. Perhaps the best surprise I've ever had. The people in the cars were the avant-guard of a squad of the National Front, Britain's self-proclaimed racists, who had turned out to protest at our commitment to this black family and at their legal victory. Leaflets were being handed to the congregation at the door inviting them to sack their 'communist vicar and maoist curate'. Placards proclaimed the same message. Even my Jewish ancestry was put forward as proof of my unworthiness to serve in the Established Church. What higher compliment could our local fascists pay us, than to turn out to damn us? Somehow our message must be getting across.

A small detachment sent by the Front's National Organiser, Martin Webster, came into our parish eucharist. I was determined that now, more than ever, the principle of a church open to all must stand. The protesters were clearly intent on interrupting my sermon. It was not the one I had prepared for that morning. I pointed out that our church really had one ultimate purpose, to share God's love with all people. We were doing our best to love our black neighbours. Today a harder challenge faced us: how do we love the members of the National Front who stand for so much we regard as evil? 'What about the police?' they shouted. 'That's easier,' I replied. 'We've already helped the police by making a small contribution to cleansing it of those who give it a bad name.'

It isn't often that a parson gets the chance to preach a dialogue sermon with those who oppose the gospel. But sermons, Anglican ones anyway, are short. I suggested we needed more time to talk to each other. Maybe that could be arranged after the service. That threw the protesters into confusion. They hoped we might have had them evicted, and had photographers on hand to record the fracas.

Peace reigned. When the service was over I insisted on photographing our visitors for the parish records. And I invited Martin Webster to return with, say, fifteen people the following

Wednesday. There would be the same number of us to listen to their ideas and to share ours with them. We hardly believed it when they actually came. It was, not surprisingly, something of a dialogue of the deaf. Even so, it was very important. Might we not be changing a few hearts and minds? These mainly very deprived young people might never have heard ideas like ours, patiently put by people who had let them talk first. Of course they couldn't admit they were wrong in each other's presence. But how many would still be with the Front two or three months later? God knows. Certainly none of them came back to our church. No startling conversion story. But a real sign that we cared for them, as well as for our black neighbours. Perhaps we should have had Bill Quaye there with us that night, or Susan or Kathleen, who today, incidentally, is an international fashion model living in Milan.

End of story? Almost. Before the National Front's exploit got in the papers – they had seen to that – I reported all that had happened to my bishop. It seemed too important for him not to know. He thought we'd made a big mistake. The members of the Front, in disrupting public worship had broken the law and should have been called to account. I should, the bishop thought, have called the police. Mervyn Stockwood was a bishop whose public ministry I greatly admired. This time I was sure he was wrong. Had they been attacking others, it might have been quite a different matter, but if the Church is under attack God's weapons of truth, justice, patience and love should suffice . . . and that doesn't exclude the expression of God's righteous anger.

Never before or after was our congregation so strong and united as on that day. Is it true then, even for the children of light, that nothing does more to keep them together than a common enemy?

If that all sounds too neat, tidy and successful, pastoral care that seemed to work, then let me at least remind myself that we did nothing to discover what help the detective who had lost his job now needed. Yes, we included him in our prayers but offered no kind of help. That it might have been rejected is irrelevant. Just as well that every communion service starts with a corporate confession of guilt. Our own. 'All have sinned and fallen short of the glory of God.'

10

The Pope's Revenge

It felt good to be one of a small band of Christian CND members, worshipping God in a zone of peace at one of the gates of the Greenham Common missile base. We were present as a sign of contradiction. We were there to affirm that, come what may, nuclear weapons could never be launched in our name or our God's. We knew we had no power to remove them. Their protectors had the power to remove us, should anything we do begin to threaten military security. And yet we sang a hymn with a refrain that declared, again and again and again: *Our God reigns!* It felt good.

The singing went on, but I fell silent. 'No, no no!' an inner voice began to shout. That's a lie. Our God does not reign. Our God has abdicated. We are living in a world of religious make-believe. This is false comfort. Our God is a failure and, like us, is only allowed to be here on sufferance. Our God is still the same God who, in Christ, stood silent and helpless before Pilate.

Crucified, risen and ascended, one with the Father and the Spirit, yes. But with what justification do we use our worldly concepts of power to turn the suffering servant of humanity into the King of Kings and Lord of Lords? The ultimate victory over the grave, the profound mystery of the triumph of love over fear, these do enable us to sing that 'the prisoner leaps to loose his chains'. There are grounds, not only for faith and love but also for hope. But there are no grounds for assuming that the world is anything other than a battleground in which the humanity of God is again and again defeated. Neither within us nor around us is there the slightest excuse for believing that God has everything under control.

An absconded God – *deus absconditus* – is a much more credible thesis. That some human beings, despite all this, have encountered the risen Christ remains the great miracle. But he meets us *incognito*. He may walk with us on our Emmaus road but, like the Bird of Heaven, we cannot grasp him, hold him, tie him down. So what do we do? We build great religious statues to him. We construct the idols of divine power that give us counterfeit confidence. And our prayer becomes unreal.

Within creation there is autonomy and within that autonomy there is given to us, who are made in God's image, a real measure of freedom. That is the limited extent of our own power. Yes, we have power. We may not like it. We may prefer to ascribe it to God. But it is ours. We are, within the complex limitations of this created order, plenipotentiaries. Limited only – yet substantially – by our total interdependence with the rest of creation and by our inherited past. We are knit into a continuum not of our individual choosing. Within that framework, we are free.

In consequence, the kind of prayer that tells God what to do is a rejection of our true role, a refusal to accept responsibility. It is not God who starts or ends wars. We do. God does not feed hungry children or let them starve. God does not rule or overrule. The world is not his puppet theatre. The praying priest in the airliner that is in danger of crashing will not avert disaster by asking God to intervene. But, even knowing that, he need not escape into the role of God's publicity agent. More is wrought by the mystery of the prayer of the loving heart than our reason can grasp. At a moment of crisis, even technological crisis, to embrace spiritually those who are at the controls is, mysteriously, to have some share in the control. To enfold both doctor and sick child in the embrace of the caring mind and the praying heart is to enter into the healing process. And, as mysteriously as our prayer is part of reality, so God, present, living, suffering and dying, is part of that reality too;

immanent and transcendent. But not, not, not a God at the controls.

If everything that happens somehow reflects what we call 'the will of God', then we would have more ground even than Job to curse, damn and reject that God. If we maintain all our religious imagery of the sovereignty of God and really think these verbal icons correspond with reality, then all moral and ethical categories turn to nonsense. Then what we call evil is as much the responsibility of that God as what we call good. Then all striving for the good ceases to make sense. For evil, for the kiss of Judas, for my own rebellion against love, I have no rational explanation. I simply accept the testimony of my mind and conscience that, at the heart of creation, there is a chronic sickness in which we all share. At the same time the life, death and resurrection of Jesus hold out the promise that there is a healing process. There is war, but at the same time there are peace negotiations. Creation groans, as creation waits to be reborn. Meanwhile in that creation God is a foreigner without even claim on the rights of a refugee. 'His own knew him not.'

I will not, therefore, fatalistically accept the status quo and ultimately ascribe it to a God who has a grand plan. We shall have to find remedies of one kind or another for the bloody mess that we have made. Remedies for cancer, a disease of our civilisation, remedies for war, also a disease of our civilisation. And personal remedies alone will not do. Epidemics are a corporate problem.

But knowing of the humility, the foolishness and indeed the helplessness of God, I am better able to cope with my own failure and to accept that of others. Sometimes I think the main advantage of being a Christian is that it removes for ever the need to save face. If God accepts failure, what need have I to pretend to be a success?

And anyway, what is success? Who is more vain than the preacher? Yet I have no evidence that my best, profoundest and most moving sermons have ever brought the Kingdom a day nearer. (Of course I am aware of the paradox – using, again and again, the 'kingdom language' when there is no king, but only a suffering servant.) Can we begin to grasp the 'majesty' of God's humility?

Humility, not timidity. Jesus, the young wandering rabbi, challenged the whole theocratic power-structure of the Temple. In first-century Jerusalem, that was Cathedral, Parliament, Law Court and Stock Exchange all in one – there was no division of power in Israel. There was only the even greater power of Rome. And – yet more paradox – because the Roman governor was weak, the Son of Man had to die. Yes, he did return. But quietly and mysteriously, with none of the triumphalism that we apparently need to boost our ecclesiastical pride and our faltering faith.

I remember how important I thought a sermon of mine was to a crowded Bristol Cathedral at the opening of the academic year. I worked and worked and overworked at it, caged the Bird of Heaven in all my academic skills and, when the day came, it all went wrong. Within minutes, I knew I'd lost the congregation, yet, I ploughed on, a prisoner of my text. 'A disaster,' I said to my host as we processed out. He nodded.

It was years later, one winter's night on a Midland railway platform with sleet in the air. A young woman appeared, as I shivered. 'Aren't you Canon Oestreicher?' I admitted it. 'I feel awful,' she said. 'I always meant to write to you. Remember that sermon you preached in Bristol Cathedral?' 'I'd rather not,' I said. 'Well, I just want you to know that it changed my whole life.' My train pulled in. She was gone.

It's seldom that we get evidence that failure is not quite what we think. More often there is nothing to redeem it, no new life springing from its ruins. Just the bleakness of rejection.

There are the spectacular failures too. At the Hyde Park Corner end of Piccadilly, where London's Hotel Intercontinental now stands, there were once grand Victorian houses. One of them, in the sixties, was occupied by hippies who, for a long time, were besieged by police. They were the object of a great deal of respectable derision. One Sunday morning I preached on the significance of their presence in the middle of

London's wealthy West End. I wondered whether Jesus might not have preferred to be with the hippies, rather than with the exclusive upper crust congregation – as it was then but happily is not now – of St James' Church in Piccadilly.

Over coffee after the Parish Communion service several of the younger parishioners challenged me. 'If you think that's where Jesus would be, why don't you go there and preach to them instead of just to us?' 'All right,' I said, 'I will. Who's coming with me?' I had more than enough volunteers. With priest and deaconess and bread and wine and our best chalice, a whole party set off from south of the river to make a foray into the Diocese of London (for which I later had to apologise to the bishop!). We got much less and much more than we had bargained for. As we approached the besieged house, with a far greater police presence than we had expected, the press swooped on us, a whole prey of reporters and photographers. Now they even had a religious angle! We were, to our embarrassment, on the front pages the next day. That's as far as we got, for the police had started evicting the squatters two hours before. Defeated, they were slowly filing out. We could only stand by and watch. And go home again.

It was a good lesson in humility for we learnt that nuns from a religious community had quietly been inside with the hippies all the while. Yet, we felt that even our arrival had not quite been a wasted sign. What might have been the ultimate put-down came from a fellow priest who had long worked in the West End and whom I greatly respected. A letter from him to me began with the memorable words: 'The ecclesiastical fool, arriving, as usual, too late . . .' That sealed our friendship.

I probably owe Hitler more than one debt of gratitude. Without him, I might not have learnt so early to be open to rejection and not to be burdened by feelings of resentment. My short but enjoyable military career never got beyond my high school's cadet corps. I was a better than average sergeant major. While still a corporal, I led a squad that was to form the firing party at the Cenotaph of my home town on Anzac Day, New Zealand's day of war remembrance. We practised hard. But a day or two before Anzac Day, 'Curly' Richards, my Latin master, apologetically took me out of the squad. 'Sorry,' he said, 'I should have known. But all the squad have to be privates.' I didn't mind. The next evening, one of the privates, my classmate Paterson, fell sick. His father phoned. Would I take his place. 'Sure,' I said, and threw my mother my uniform-jacket and asked her to take off the stripes, so I'd look like a private.

When I turned up the next morning with the others, Mr Richards, in his captain's uniform, went pale. He took me aside and told me the truth. The President of the RSA, the veteran's association, had threatened a demonstration if 'that German' was in the firing party. Would I please go home quietly and make no fuss? I'd long ago learnt that life wasn't fair and rode my bike home whistling. I'd learnt early too to tell the difference between what people do and what they say. On the radio that very day the self-same President of the RSA spoke of reconciliation and forgiveness, of building one new world on the ruins of the past. All of sixteen years old, I smiled the smile of wisdom and was quietly proud of having been sent home.

Next morning at school assembly our principled headmaster told the school what had happened. 'Our school will either get an apology, or I resign from the RSA.' I went to his office to thank him. 'Oestreicher,' he said sternly, 'this has nothing to do with you. Get lost.' He knew the dangers of pride.

It was a bit different when other New Zealanders did it again, some forty years later. '*Oestreicher rejected*' was the headline on the *Guardian's* front page in London. In one sense, what more could a Christian want! But it really wasn't easy; to be persuaded, after much agonising and prayer, to return to New Zealand as a bishop, then to be elected, and then, apparently on the basis of rumour and innuendo and misinformation, to be vetoed by a series of committees who had little idea of what it was all about. That wasn't easy. But the pain did not lie – as most people assumed – in the publicity, in losing face, in being made to look foolish. It lay in not being allowed to do what I felt I had been called to do; to serve the community that a generation before had given refuge and a new life to my parents and to me.

A fellow priest, who had worked hard to get me elected, reflected that such a rejection was – despite the obvious difference – 'the Jesus experience'. I wonder. Would that I really were the Christian radical that those committees thought they were saying no to! Jesus deserved to be crucified. It was not a mistake. I'd like to think I deserved that kind of rejection. There's a poster stemming from the 'confessing church' in South Africa, from those who will not conform to apartheid. It asks the pertinent question: 'If you were charged with being a Christian, would there be enough evidence to convict you?' I think I'd have to say no. The only comforting thought is that, even after Peter's denial of his Lord, he was allowed to remain the chief apostle. That, I imagine, makes it possible to remain a committed Roman Catholic, even after reading an uncensored history of the papacy. Where would any of us be, without the miracle of free grace?

Be it as a result of our own failure, or of our deserved or undeserved rejection by others, are we right always to accept the consequence as 'the will of God'? I think not. For that assumes a divine blueprint, constantly under revision. It does suggest that the world is God's stage, that he has written the libretto and that when we sing wrong notes, he'll adjust the music and rewrite the text. No, we have been given a mind and a conscience. History is the wise and the unwise, the moral and the immoral record of how we direct our wills. God somehow is within that process, not an outside observer, giving good and bad marks. God is mysteriously present within the wholeness and the brokenness of our being; God in our successes and God in our failures. God in our health and in our disease. God, as the dying John Robinson was able to affirm in a last hopeful sermon, 'God in my cancer too'. God dying and living with us.

So, was God's will fulfilled or frustrated in my not being confirmed as Bishop of Wellington? It is the wrong question, because I doubt if God was concerned with it at all. God – it

seems – really has delegated decision-making to us, uncon-
ditionally. What is of spiritual and moral importance is how I
live with whatever decision is made. Whether I live or die at a
particular time may depend on my diet or the current state of
medical science or of traffic conditions. None of these are 'in
God's hands'. *How* we live or die is quite another matter and
the one where we need each other, where we need God's
presence (whether or not we're aware of it), where we need
all the human and divine resources that exist.

If nothing is divinely 'programmed', what of salvation
history? What of the birth and death and resurrection of Jesus?
What of the 'Durham debate'? Was Pilate 'programmed' and
not free to let Jesus go? If so, then he bears no responsibility
and was right to wash his hands. The birth and death and
resurrection of Jesus were, I believe, no more inevitable than
any other part of history. What then of what we call miracles?
Existence itself, and the mind that can reflect on it, is the
ultimate miracle. Within that framework we perceive events to
be ordinary or extraordinary. Both are real. Is it not mildly
ludicrous for our finite minds to want to penetrate the mystery
of an immanent and a transcendent God beyond that point?

Of course the virgin birth and the empty tomb are possible.
But if they should ever be proved to be human constructs, aids
to faith, pious legends, what difference could that possibly
make to our experience of the living Christ, of the love that
will not let us go?

Thank God for a bishop with the inner freedom to be an
enfant terrible. The Church of England will die of spiritual
boredom before it dies of heresy. But having played his creative
theological games, the heir to the princely bishopric of Durham,
living in Auckland Castle, knows well that the Parable of the
Last Judgement will judge him and each of us and also our
apostate nation. Dives might well have been a 'sound Catholic'
or a 'devout Evangelical'. Lazarus might well have been
neither. But the poor man is in the Kingdom. Let bishops be
doctrinally safely orthodox or wildly speculative. The Spirit –
and ordinary people too – will judge them by their love. And

not only bishops! Love is about bread and peace and the preservation of God's creation.

Those great issues give us much ground for despair. Hunger, torture and war remain endemic. Amnesty International's work is a growth industry. Dan Berrigan's vision of a fellowship of human beings skilled in the simple art of reading the gospel and living according to its faith is more needed now than ever. Openness to failure is essential if despair is not to undo all that is good. And – it is important to remember – despair assails us even more often in the small things than in the great. In thirteen years of parish ministry I failed to transform that parish into a power-house of the Kingdom. Yes, there are some parishes that fit that description. Go to the Roman Catholic Church of Our Lady of the Wayside in Solihull, and see what I mean. But I don't carry around a burden of guilt that I'm not Pat O'Mahoney.

Yet I still quietly suffer because, when a group of my most creative and prophetic colleagues and friends, for want of patience and humour, fell out with our bishop on account of his insensitivity to their vision, my attempts to reconcile them ended in both sides feeling I had betrayed them and the truth. There was no easy cure to the bitterness and the pain that caused. Those are the real heart-break failures; and the even more shattering insight that I was too busy or too tired to comfort a sick child or to sit through hours of despair with an alcoholic tramp. When guilt eats into our soul, then, but for the love that will not let us go, we would be lost.

Will Christians learn to embrace their failures? Is a penitent Church a possibility? Church history suggests that the possibilities are remote. How we relish our minor triumphs, specially over our opponents! Pyrrhic victories. In the heart of East Berlin there survives the beautiful medieval parish Church of St Mary. (So much better than the triumphalist cathedral the Kaiser built a few hundred yards away and recently rebuilt at the behest of the Communist authorities.) St Mary's is topped by a small cross. It stands in the shadow of East Berlin's best piece of modern architecture, its elegant television tower, beaming out programmes that hardly anyone watches, because, for reasons good and bad, the Western channels are so much more popular. The TV tower has, high up, a rotating restaurant looking down on divided Berlin. Reflecting metal discs surround the restaurant in its globe. When the sun shines on it, from whatever angle, a bright cross, as though it were planned in neon light, shines out over Berlin. So embarrassing was it for the Party leadership – so rumour has it – that the Politburo met to discuss whether the discs should be covered in non-reflecting paint. Berliners nicknamed the TV tower 'the Pope's Revenge'.

Christians enjoy that. Germans call it *Schadenfreude*. It puts the Party in its place. It even suggests a witty piece of heavenly planning – communist Berlin overlooked and overruled by a glittering cross. A nice piece of fantasy, but not the only way to read the signs. Might the symbol of the double cross not point to a different kind of divine humour, one that puts both Church and State in their place: a small, modest, almost hidden cross on St Mary's church-tower; a bolder, much more inescapable cross, a mass-media cross, towering over it and symbolising the effects both of the power and of the powerlessness of worldly authority. While we play games with such signs, the Bird of Heaven performs her wonders on both sides of the Berlin Wall, with or without the Church.

11

The Feast of St Michael

If life – and especially Christian life – is a constant paradox, is living day by day with contradictions, where every truth conceals a lie and every lie a truth, it is all the more important to discover a still, clear centre where nothing is confused, a mystery at the heart of creation that is beyond paradox and to which the soul can respond in freedom.

The discovery of the one thing that really matters, the inner journey towards ultimate reality, has no prescribed route. The deep wells of the water of life are to be found in many different places. The same divine truth will be perceived by every created being in a unique way.

Those whom the mystery of life has enabled to walk some way with Jesus will each have encountered their own Saviour, yet the same Lord. For each of us, as the paradoxes give way to ultimate simplicity, it will become clear that the closer we come to what this Jesus called the Kingdom, the more deeply we will believe in less and less. Only love in the end will be left. Even to put that into words is already to begin to confuse the issue, to muddy the water.

Every kind of spirituality will say that differently. The mystic will not want to say it at all. The disciple will not need to. She will simply share her bread or hold the hand of a dying beggar. The satirist will shoot down every dogmatic assertion and the jester will make the last paradox explode into laughter. The child will expose the nakedness of the richly apparelled prelate and the mother will wipe away the tears of the last guru whose self-confident panaceas have burst like bubbles in the wind. The rich will have time to crown their children with dandelions.

Like the richer poor. And the experts in prayer will know, on behalf of the rest of us, how to explain all that to God.

Thanks to a beautiful girl in New Zealand, on my eighteenth birthday, on the Feast of St Michael the Archangel 1949, in a small Dunedin church dedicated to Michael and all God's other messengers (as is Coventry Cathedral in which I now work), I first met Jesus early in the morning in the breaking of bread, in Holy Communion. My journey inwards that day took the turning that led to one kind of priesthood. I already knew the Jesus who had blinded Saul on the Damascus Road with a great light, for that Jesus had brought my own agnostic Jewish father to baptism. And I had known the Holy Spirit, the Inner Light, as she is corporately experienced in the shared silence of Quaker worship. To that Spirit, affirming, as the main-line churches fail to do, the priesthood of all believers, I returned much later in life, not renouncing my particular priesthood but rooting it even more firmly in the universal priesthood that the Son of Man shares with the whole human family.

That men and women should share equally in that priesthood, both in its universality and its particularity, is surely true. That the greater part of Christendom – including the Church of England – is not yet willing to recognise that fact reflects that in most respects the life of the Church is guided by the principle that no change is normal while change is exceptional. On that principle slavery went unchallenged for some eighteen hundred years of 'Christian' history; after all St Paul had not been against it. St Paul serves a male-dominated theology equally well, and – in my view – with equal irrelevance, if the presence of the Holy Spirit is taken seriously. A Church hiding behind scripture and tradition to disguise from itself its fear of life has simply not heard its Lord saying to the synagogue: 'You have heard it said . . . but I say unto you.' Liberal and Reformed Judaism has stolen a march on that Church, as has the best of a caring, secular world. The recurring tragedy of Christian history is that the Church, called by its Lord to be in the world but not of it, has, more often than not, been of the world but not in it.

What does Michael, the Archangel, symbolise? In the words of a hymn: 'God at war with human wrong.' One of the profounder paradoxes of Christian faith is that the Prince of Peace declared that he had come not to bring peace, but a sword. In its long history Christendom has generally preferred to turn its sword on the enemies of the status quo, the enemies of the powerful and the rich, the enemies of ecclesiastical authority. By doing that, the Church has turned its sword on its own Lord. The devil is seldom to be found at his most insidious in the enemy camp but in the Church's own. Where are the roots of Auschwitz? In centuries of anti-semitic theology. Where are the roots of atheistic communism? In centuries of ecclesiastical collusion with the oppressors of the poor.

To change the imagery: the Church has seldom been absorbed by the world as salt is absorbed, giving it a new taste. It has usually been happy to be the world's icing sugar, somewhat sweetening the intolerable and changing nothing.

To be a Christian in the Church today is consciously to share that guilt, to carry that self-inflicted cross. The cross of our own spiritual bankruptcy. No chic radicalism can purge that guilt. For Western Christians to embrace 'liberation theology' without sacrificial involvement in the liberation struggle in a particular place, with all its moral ambiguities, is simply to side with tomorrow's power structures instead of today's; no more than a good social and psychological insurance policy. Icons of Oscar Romero on walls in England or New England are not passports to the Kingdom.

But the Church is not irretrievably lost, God's humiliation is not irreversible. Although most of the time most of us have to live *etsi deus non daretur* – as though there was no God – there are signs of the resurrection in us and around us. People are capable of loving and of being loved. The hungry women of Moscow, their sons dead, put bread into the hands of broken, starving German prisoners of war as they were humiliatingly herded through the streets of the Soviet capital, when Hitler's dreams lay in ruins. Franz Jägerstetter, faithful Catholic peasant, defied bishops and generals and said yes to the guillotine, rather than fight in Hitler's unjust war. Mother Maria and Maximilian Kolbe, Orthodox nun and Catholic friar, took the place of Jews and died in their stead in Hitler's death camps.

The title of Leo Tolstoy's short story, 'Where love is, God is', really says it all; for God is love. Never will I be trapped in the kind of Christian 'orthodoxy' which suggests that only those with the 'right belief' are 'saved', whatever that strange word means. If it means anything, we are saved not because of what *we* do or believe but because God's self-emptying, self-giving, self-sacrificing love will not let us go. That some of us, some of the time, are actually aware of that, is miracle enough.

And it is a fearsome thought. What are we doing when we turn our back on that love? One answer is to be found in the Parable of the Last Judgement. To the just, God says: 'I was hungry and you fed me, thirsty and you gave me to drink, a stranger and you took me in, naked and you clothed me, in prison and you visited me.' The unjust did not. And who is this God? My friend, my child, my enemy and even me.

If that was the whole truth, there would be no gospel, no good news. But the same God in Christ, nailed to a tree, prayed for those who were killing him. That is the ultimate miracle.

My experience of life tells me that not only Christians, and sometimes Christians last of all, are signs of crucified and risen life. Thank God no spiritual élite has been given a monopoly on living for others. My old communist friend James Klugmann, with whom I edited *What Kind of Revolution?* in the sixties, called himself an atheist. He was closer to the heart of Jesus than I have ever been. He, like Jesus, was a man for others. Card-carrying Tories are not beyond the reach of the Holy Spirit either. As history shows, not even popes and archbishops are. To miracles there is no end.

Have I – in that last paragraph – confusingly 'strayed into a world of politics'? Surely, many will want to say, these spiritual insights are too sublime to be tainted by our squalid human conflicts. I wonder. Usually that Parable of the Last Judgement is read as God speaking to the individual soul. And it is telling, when read that way. But how does it begin? 'When the Son of

Man comes in his glory . . . before him will be gathered *all the nations* and he will separate them, one from another as a shepherd separates the sheep from the goats . . .'

If that is true, then there is no escape from politics. If the hungry are to be fed and the oppressed set free it is a matter for the nations as well as for each child of God. Love is in large measure about justice. And justice is about economics and politics. Where we invest our money has everything to do with the Kingdom of God. How America and Britain and France and Germany treat their immigrant labour force qualifies them all for condemnation. They deplore apartheid and go on profiting from it, and God is not fooled. Of course there are practical differences, but in the end no valid line can ever be drawn between the personal and the political. They constantly reflect each other. Both glory and betrayal. They stand and fall together. And are saved together. For all his wisdom, Reinhold Niebuhr's central thesis in *Moral Man and Immoral Society* is not sustainable in either theory or practice. The Archangel's war with the devil will always be both personal and political. It is the interaction of the one with the other that truly makes us human beings and also makes God God. That prophetic priest and pastor in London's East End between the wars, Father St John Groser, expressed this with simple clarity in his pastoral memoirs, *Persons and Politics*, published soon after World War II.

Here then, to conclude these reflections of a reluctant priest and an uneasy Quaker, are five of my own experiences of ecumenical pastoralia that have helped to convince me that, on the long road to the Kingdom, persons and politics are one, just as God, in three 'persons', is One.

In the aftermath of the Soweto riots of 1976 it was my rewarding and painful task – while Chairman of Amnesty International in Britain – to gather evidence of imprisonment and torture in South Africa and Namibia. My meetings with victims and the families of those who had died was moving, heart-rending and in the end, a source of hope. For all the misery and degradation a struggle for liberation is always also inspiring. Yet what I shall remember most, and what remained at the heart of my prayers, were two meetings with men in the camp of the oppressor.

In Windhoek, capital of occupied Namibia, I stayed with my friends in the front line of the Church's struggle against South African oppression. But I wanted to meet other Christians too. Could I go, I asked, to meet a Minister of the pro-apartheid Dutch Reformed Church? My hosts were astonished. Yes, they said. We know who they are. We know where they live. But you will have to go on your own. We would neither wish to go, nor would we be welcome. So I went to one of them, the one who would be most likely to talk to me. When he realised who and what I was, I saw fear in his eyes. He shepherded his family out and then asked me in. I would do him a disservice were I now, even a decade later, to name him.

Tears were in his eyes, that I had come. It was as though I had agreed to visit and embrace a leper. He did not say very much. But he left me in no doubt that he knew the truth and suffered because of what his Church and his *Volk* were doing. He had not had the inner strength to leave Afrikanerdom, to go with or without his family into spiritual exile, as a few great prophets, whose greatness he recognised, had done. He asked me to pray with him and for his family and for his Afrikaner tribe. And when I went he hoped I would not be seen. The 'Christian world' has neither prayed resolutely enough for this man and his people nor fought resolutely enough against the things that they are doing. We have neither loved the sinner enough nor hated the sin enough. That is part of the measure of our involvement in the guilt of South Africa.

My other meeting, no less personal, no less political, was with the Chief Secretary of South Africa's Ministry of External Affairs, another of that land's many Bothas. A representative of oppressive power. From him there came no fragments of penitence but, for the best part of a morning, the sane and civilised defence of the insane and barbaric. What made it so disturbing was not its cynicism but its sincerity. Here was a man more willing than I to assert the saving grace of God, yet serving – in my eyes – the very devil. If God does so little to defend his children from such heresy, who is this God of mine? Never does the unsolved mystery of evil bring me closer to denying the power of love than when confronted by the love of power posing as God's justice. I did not hate that man – and I think he felt it – and I hope I would not, even if I were his prisoner. But I have a quarrel that is both intensely personal and deeply political with the God whom both he and I claim to worship. That quarrel only ends when I stop and hear a man, nailed to a tree, praying: 'Father forgive them, for they know not what they do.'

Heinz Brandt, who died early in 1986, was the kind of man most people tend to call a saint, though that would have made him shudder. After World War II he was one of the architects of the communist trade union movement in East Germany. By the mid fifties he was disillusioned by what Stalinism had done and was still doing. This was not his idea of a people's democracy. Sadly, he left the GDR and came West; not to campaign against the East but to help build socialism with a human face in the West. Adenauer's Bonn was no more to his liking than Ulbricht's Berlin. But in the latter he was regarded as a traitor. In a sense he was, though an honourable one.

In the late fifties he visited West Berlin and was somehow spirited, kidnapped, to East Berlin. There, in secret, he was tried and sentenced to a long prison term. Amnesty International campaigned for his release. Canon John Collins, founder of CND and much respected in Eastern Europe, took me with him when he went to East Berlin to plead for Brandt's release. Party leader Walter Ulbricht agreed to meet us. He listened to our case for Brandt's release and then told us in no uncertain terms why this traitor had got all he deserved. Ulbricht finished with a question: 'Why do you two priests compromise your work for peace by pleading for this scoundrel? If he were a Christian it might be your duty but what is he? A traitor to communism.' Our sermon to Walter Ulbricht was masterfully short. 'He is a human being. Is that not enough?'

Here again, in an almost classic confrontation with power, and also with the weakness of power, was the intimate unity between the personal and the political. One of my sadder reflections on that experience is that all too many Christians agree with Walter Ulbricht, the Communist. When a Christian suffers injustice, Christians should come to the rescue. When a Communist suffers injustice, it is none of their business. Tribal mentality. To this no one has given a better answer than Martin Niemöller, the leader of Protestant resistance to Hitler and for eight years Hitler's 'special prisoner'. On his release Niemöller said: 'First they came for the Communists and I did nothing. Then they came for the Jews and I did nothing. Then they came for the Liberals and I did nothing. Then they came for me and it was too late.'

But even Niemöller's reflection is not the last word. All those he listed were innocent victims. But even the guilty are human beings. To remain silent when they are tortured and misused may bring no obvious evil in its train. And yet humanity is debased. So today, not only should the world be crying for the release of Sakharov and Mandela but also of old, sick and guilty Rudolf Hess, once Hitler's deputy, a prisoner since 1941, alone in the bizarre isolation of Spandau Prison. If he dies in captivity, a fragment of fascist inhumanity will have triumphed, for Hess would have shown no mercy either. The gospel knows of justice. Of retribution it knows nothing.

In 1968, while napalm was burning up the villages and the children of Vietnam, a dream died in Czechoslovakia. A popular, humane, perhaps too idealistic communist experiment was killed by Soviet tanks. The life of the Czechs and the Slovaks was, as the invaders put it, 'normalised'. How the ordinary people felt, the whole world knew and even the Soviet tank crews learnt to their astonishment, having been conned into believing they were coming as liberators.

Two months later, before the frontiers were closed to people like me, I paid a nostalgic farewell visit to what remained of the 'Prague Spring'. It was rush hour in the early evening in the old part of the city. I waited to cross a crowded pedestrian crossing, stepped out and quickly stepped back. Coming at great speed towards the crossing down a narrow one-way street was a Soviet jeep, one soldier perched on it, driving as though he were on the steppes of central Asia and expecting the people to get out of his way. They didn't. They slowed their steps. They were in no mood to let him pass. Dangerously late, he realised what was going to happen and braked so sharply that the jeep spun around twice on its axis and came to a halt side-on, just feet short of the crossing. His engine had stalled. He sat, terrified, shaking. He looked like a frightened child. The people on the crossing cut him dead. It was a kind of spiritual lynching. My mind went to Belfast, and not just there. In many places in our world it might well have been a physical lynching. It was frightening, a piece of live street theatre from which I wanted to get away; I began to cross the street again. Coming from the other side, one face stood out from the angry, sullen crowd, the sad face of a beautiful young woman. I would have stopped to look at that face at any time, but at this moment specially, a welcome escape. She, and only she, was looking at the young soldier. As she passed me, his eyes met hers. She smiled. He was alive again. Started his jeep, and drove on.

I had experienced a moment of crossed-out hate. The young woman was probably unaware of the significance of what she had done. She had revealed that she was a human being first, and a Czech only after that. Some people think of that as treason. For me it was a sign of the glorious liberty of a child of God. I would like to think that young woman was a Christian. I suspect, were she to read these lines now and vaguely remember, she would just shake her head and smile, as she smiled then.

Windhoek, Pretoria, Berlin, Prague and finally –
    Auschwitz. I did not really want to go. I had been to enough former concentration camps turned into museums of horror.

Could I face the mountains of human hair, of discarded spectacles and even of children's toys? And then the gas chambers? Here, some of my father's relatives had died. To avoid this end, the grandmother I had loved most, had taken her own life. I went, yet not only out of courtesy to my Polish hosts. A medical student who spoke good English was my guide. It was her holiday job. She did it well, without the usual heavy pathos. And without the anti-fascist slogans. Why waste words here?

When we had seen it all, the places where millions had died, each uniquely loved, she showed me the grave where one more lay buried. The Nazi commandant, whom they had hanged. Justice. But I remembered Vicky's cartoon on the day Eichmann, who had ordered these murders, who was the commandant's boss, was due to be sentenced in Jerusalem. It showed Eichmann in his bullet-proof glass dock, surrounded by his victims. Under the drawing Vicky, the Jew, had written: 'Brothers, kill no more.' Wisdom, that blew away in the wind. One more had to die. This was justice, but not redemption.

We walked out of the camp enclosure into a reception room for visitors. A huge book, already full of comments, was put in front of me. 'Please write in it what you feel.' I read some of the many expressions of horror and anger and shame. I felt none of them. I could only, without words, try to pray and then write the timeless words 'Father forgive'. My student guide took one look, shook her head and walked away. Was that not a kind of blasphemy? To forgive *that*? Some spiritual kind of double cross?